The Pocket Essential

FREUD & PSYCHOANALYSIS

T401

UGH   COLLEGE

www.pocketessentials.com

First published in Great Britain 2001 by Pocket Essentials, 18 Coleswood Road,
Harpenden, Herts, AL5 1EQ

Distributed in the USA by Trafalgar Square Publishing, PO Box 257, Howe Hill
Road, North Pomfret, Vermont 05053

Copyright © Nick Rennison 2001
Series Editor: Nick Rennison

A CIP catalogue record for this book is available from the British Library.

ISBN 1-903047-54-4

2 4 6 8 10 9 7 5 3 1

Book typeset by Pdunk
Printed and bound by Cox & Wyman

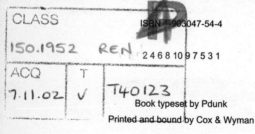

CONTENTS

Chapter One: Freud's Life

Early Life

Sigmund Freud was born on the 6th May 1856 in the small country town of Freiberg, then part of the Austro-Hungarian Empire, now the Moravian town of Pribor in the Czech Republic. He was the eldest son of Jacob Freud, a relatively unsuccessful and unprosperous Jewish merchant, and Jacob's second wife, Amalia who had married the previous year. Amalia was twenty years younger than her husband and Jacob had two adult sons from a previous marriage who were much the same age as their stepmother. Freud's earliest playmates included the children of one of these sons, Emanuel. That uncle, nephew and niece were roughly contemporaries, as were Freud's mother and his two older half-brothers, must have caused generational (and, possibly, sexual) confusion in the young Freud's mind and biographers have felt free to speculate on the influence this may have had on his future interest in childhood sexuality and its effects on adult life. In an age, however, when many women died young in childbirth and many widowers married second wives much younger than themselves, the Freud household's complex interrelationships would not have been significantly uncommon.

A year after Sigmund's arrival in the world, Amalia Freud gave birth to another boy, who was named Julius, but he died when only a few months old. In 1858 a sister Anna was born and she was followed at almost yearly intervals by four more girls. Alexander, Freud's youngest sibling, was born in 1866. Sigmund, the talented oldest sibling, was to grow up surrounded by adoring and admiring females, convinced of his special genius. Most important of these was, of course, his mother who lavished her attention on her first-born and was his earliest teacher. In later life, Freud wrote, 'A man who has been the indisputable favourite of his mother keeps for life the feeling of a conqueror, that confidence of success that often induces real success.' It is clear that when he wrote this he was thinking of his own position as his mother's golden boy.

The Freud family, in the late 1850s, was not thriving in Freiberg. In 1859 Freud's parents considered moving and travelled briefly to Leipzig to assess the potential of that city. Jacob's sons from his first marriage uprooted themselves and their families and moved to England. In 1860 Jacob made the less dramatic decision to move to Vienna, the imperial capital. It was to remain Freud's home until the Nazis drove him into exile in London in 1938.

In 1865 Freud, hitherto taught at home and at a private school, was enrolled at the Leopoldstadter Realgymnasium. In the eight years he attended the school he proved himself a star pupil, showing a gift for both languages and sciences, and regularly emerging top of his class. The promise of greatness that his parents, particularly his mother, had always detected in him was given full encouragement. Although the family remained relatively impoverished, and lived in restricted circumstances, Sigmund always had his own room for study and nothing was allowed to stand in the way of his academic progress. On one well-known occasion, which reflects less well on the budding genius than the early biographers who recorded it seem to have thought, Freud complained about the piano-playing of one of his sisters, which was disturbing his concentration. The piano was removed.

In 1873 Freud completed his triumphal school progress by graduating with distinction and was ready to enter the University of Vienna. He had long toyed with the idea of studying law but lectures he had attended on Goethe and on Darwin had changed his thinking and it was the medical faculty that Freud joined. His medical studies engaged him until 1881, several years longer than was usual, and it is clear from both his letters at the time and the work that he undertook that his aim was to be a research scientist rather than a practising doctor. He studied under the eminent German physiologist Ernst Brücke, later working as an assistant in the Physiological Institute Brücke, and in 1876 he won a research scholarship to the laboratory of Marine Zoology. While at Trieste he produced the first of the many publications that were to bear his name over the following sixty years – a paper on the sexual organs of eels.

Freud's hopes of a career in pure science were dashed by a combination of personal circumstances and larger social issues. His father's often shaky finances had been dealt a severe blow by a downturn in the Austrian economy and Freud was only too well aware of the need to earn his own money. As a Jew, advancement in the discreetly anti-Semitic world of academe would be difficult. In addition, in 1881 (the year he qualified as a doctor of medicine) Freud had fallen in love with Martha Bernays. If he were to marry her, he needed to find some career ladder less uncertain than that offered by research. Private practice seemed the best option but to enter private practice he needed to undertake another prolonged period of training at the Vienna General Hospital. At first he worked as an assistant to Herman Nothnagel, the Professor of Internal Medicine but, in 1883, Freud had his first encounter with medical psychiatry when he worked for five months at the psychiatric clinic run by Theodor Meynert. His time at Meynert's clinic persuaded him that his future lay with diseases of the mind and the nervous system.

Cocaine and Charcot

It was at this time that he began his friendship with Josef Breuer. Breuer, fourteen years older than Freud, was already a respected Viennese physician and physiologist. Like most of Freud's close friendships, that with Breuer was to end in estrangement and disillusion, but the older man was to stake his claim as the grandfather of psychoanalysis when he told Freud of the 'talking cure' he had used, with varying degrees of success, on the patient later known as 'Anna O.' (See Chapter Four) At the time the case may have seemed to Freud no more than an interesting curiosity but he was to return to it in later years and attempt to persuade an increasingly uncomfortable Breuer of its wider significance.

It was also during these years that Freud undertook his experiments with the medicinal use of cocaine. In later life he was keen to disassociate himself from these researches as far as possible but, at the time, he was clearly convinced that he had stumbled on a wonder drug and that cocaine was to be his road to fame and fortune. He took it himself. He prescribed it to his fiancée Martha Bernays. When his father had to undergo an eye operation, Freud not only insisted that cocaine be used as a local anaesthetic but assisted in the operation himself. Luckily another Viennese doctor, Carl Koller, laid prior claim to the discovery of the medicinal uses of cocaine. Freud could congratulate himself on a narrow escape from professional ignominy. By the late 1880s the addictive nature of the drug was becoming clear. Indeed, to Freud's continuing self-reproach, one of his friends, Ernst Fleischl-Marxow, who had first taken cocaine at Freud's recommendation, had become a confirmed addict and later committed suicide. (Freud may have been unnecessarily self-punishing about his role in his friend's fate. Fleischl-Marxow was already a despairing morphine addict when he first took cocaine and it is clear from contemporary accounts that he was not a man destined to make old bones.)

Whilst he was busy promulgating the virtues of cocaine, Freud's life had taken a number of decisive new turns. In 1885 he became a Privat Docent (a kind of junior lecturer) at the University of Vienna, teaching a course on neuropathology. That same year he was given a small grant that enabled him to travel to Paris and study at the Saltpêtrière asylum there. Freud was lonely during his time in Paris and wrote a number of uncharacteristically self-pitying letters to Martha Bernays and others, detailing his difficulties in accustoming himself to Paris and his inability to persuade Parisians that he was speaking comprehensible French. (Later travellers may well sympathise.) However, from a professional perspective, his visit was invaluable. The director of the Saltpêtrière was Jean Martin Charcot who was then the best-known neurologist in the world. Charcot specialised in the study of hysteria. He had put forward a number of controversial theories about the nature of hysteria which was then assumed either to be a collection of strange phenomena brought on by disturbances in the female sexual organs or mere play-acting by attention-seeking women. Charcot denied that hysteria was exclusively female and, demonstrating that hysterical symptoms could be induced under hypnotism, claimed that it was a neurological rather than a physical problem. This was progress but Charcot refused to countenance the idea that hysteria might have its roots in psychological difficulties or that hypnotism could have any general benefit as a means of treatment.

Freud was enormously impressed by Charcot (he later named his eldest son after him) and what he had seen at the Saltpêtrière. When he returned to Vienna he translated Charcot's Lectures on the Diseases of the Nervous System and, in October 1886, he delivered a lecture himself to the Vienna Medical Society on the subject of Male Hysteria. This proved a mistake. To the average Viennese doctor of the time the idea of male hysteria was almost as laughable as the idea of male pregnancy. The very word came from the Greek 'hystera', meaning 'womb'. Freud was derided and retired to lick his wounds. Vienna was not yet ready for Charcot's more advanced ideas, let alone the even more radical theories that Freud had half-glimpsed behind them.

Marriage and Hysteria

Despite the failure of his lecture, Freud had much to occupy him. On his return from Paris he had opened a private medical practice specialising in nervous disorders. In September of 1886, after a four-year engagement, he had finally felt able to marry Martha Bernays. He was launched on a new era in both his personal and professional life. The idea of using hypnotism as a form of therapy had not left him. In late 1887 he wrote to his friend Wilhelm Fliess, 'I have thrown myself into hypnosis in the last few weeks and achieved all sorts of small but curious successes.' His attention was also drawn to the work of another Frenchman, Hippolyte Bernheim, who seemed to have shown that, despite what Charcot might believe, the power of suggestion could be used as treatment. Freud also remembered Breuer's case of Anna O. in which the patient had clearly benefited, at least briefly, from the use of hypnosis.

Wilhelm Fliess, the friend to whom he wrote of his experiments in hypnosis, was to become Freud's closest intellectual confidant over the next ten years. Both men tended to see themselves as lonely pioneers, ostracised by their peers because of the adventurousness and progressiveness of their ideas. (A cruel historical judgement on Fliess' ideas might be that they were not so much adventurous as half-baked but Freud, for many years, continued to give at least lip-service to the notion of Fliess' genius.) Fliess, two years younger than Freud, was a Berlin nose-and-throat specialist who held eccentric beliefs about 23-day and 28-day 'cycles' of health and about supposed deep-rooted connections between the nose and the sexual organs. Today Fliess may seem like little more than a crank but he provided crucial intellectual support for Freud at a critical time in the latter's life and Freud used his letters to Fliess as a means of sounding out new ideas.

Slowly Freud was moving towards the belief that hysteria and hysterical symptoms originated in childhood sexual trauma. He based this belief both on his practical experience of hysterical patients (throughout the late 1880s and early 1890s he saw many such patients and was refining his use of hypnosis and the 'talking cure' first adopted by Breuer) and on the theoretical system he was beginning to construct. Josef Breuer continued to be Freud's increasingly reluctant co-worker. Breuer was uneasy about Freud's insistence on the importance of sexuality in the origin of hysteria but was persuaded to collaborate on a book, *Studies in Hysteria*, which was published in 1895. By the time the book appeared Breuer had had enough and the friendship with Freud cooled noticeably.

With his growing family (he was to have six children, the youngest Anna being born in 1895) Freud had moved, in 1891, to Berggasse 19, which was to be his home and consulting rooms until he left Austria in 1938. It was in Berggasse that, increasingly aware of the limitations of hypnotism, he began to treat patients on the couch that has become such a permanent part of psychoanalytic folklore. By sitting out of sight of the patient, applying gentle pressure to the forehead and encouraging them to talk about what was passing through their minds, Freud found that he could bring the patients' repressed memories back to the surface.

The Emergence of Psychoanalysis

Between the publication of *Studies in Hysteria* in 1895 and *The Interpretation of Dreams* in late 1899 (the book was post-dated to the following year when published), the cornerstones of psychoanalytic theory were put in place. Hypnosis and suggestion were replaced by free association and the study of dreams. In an article for a scholarly journal Freud first made use of the term 'psychoanalysis'. Freud undertook his own self-analysis, using the techniques he had employed on his patients, particularly the study of his dreams. The death of his father in 1896 affected Freud profoundly and several of his own dreams that he used to important effect in *The Interpretation of Dreams* included appearances by Jacob. Most importantly, and later controversially, Freud changed his ideas about the reality of the childhood sexual experiences his patients were revealing.

In 1896 Freud still believed that his patients were recovering memories of real events. In a lecture to a scientific society, received as unenthusiastically as most of his lectures on his own theories were at that time, he stated that, 'at the bottom of every case of hysteria there are one or more occurrences of premature sexual experience.' Just over a year later, in September 1897, he was writing to Fliess that he had abandoned his 'seduction' theory. Patients were not reporting real memories of sexual abuse but fantasies of sexual activity. The central role in the genesis of neuroses was played not by sexual trauma inflicted as a child but by the fantasy to which childhood sexual feelings gave rise.

Today this intellectual volte-face has proved one of the most controversial of all aspects of Freud's life. Many critics, most notably Jeffrey Masson, have accused Freud of turning his back on the genuine suffering of his largely women patients, refusing to believe the stories of abuse they were telling him and insisting that they were solely imaginary. Why did Freud change his mind? Despite what the most vociferous critics say, it is difficult to believe that he did it because he could not face the idea of widespread child abuse that his original theory revealed or that he feared the continuing opposition of his professional peers. As his whole life shows he had an extraordinarily tough and resolute intellect that followed where the evidence appeared to lead him – even into deeply taboo territory – and he was unafraid of the role of lonely pioneer. Freud changed his mind because he believed he had discovered evidence that repressed sexual fantasies about parents and parental figures existed in everyone. One of the principal factors in convincing him of this was his own self-analysis and interpretation of his own dreams.

These crucial years of the late 1890s, outwardly lacking in major incident but marked by the central intellectual journey of Freud's life, also saw the emergence of what remains the most widely known of his ideas – what is popularly known as 'the Freudian slip'. Freud was becoming increasingly certain that unconscious processes were the driving forces behind the human mind and that even apparently simple acts of, say, forgetting were the result of mechanisms of which the conscious mind was unaware. In 1898 he published an article called 'The Psychical Mechanism of Forgetting' which again drew on his own experience (of forgetting the name of a renaissance artist) to highlight these unconscious processes.

Freud spent the summer of the following year away from Vienna, completing *The Interpretation of Dreams*, to many people his most important book and the one in which he most fully described his method of analysing dreams to reveal the workings of the unconscious. To Freud, dreams had become 'the royal road to the unconscious' and his book was a detailed map of the twists and turns the road took. As he acknowledged in later years it was also something else. 'For me this book has a further and subjective meaning which I was only able to understand after its completion. It proved itself to be a part of my self-analysis, my reaction to the death of my father, that is, to the most significant event, the deepest loss in a man's life.' Freud hoped that the book would be his own royal road to fame and recognition but it received scant attention and the few reviews were largely negative. His position continued to be, as he said, one of 'splendid isolation.'

The Wednesday Group and Early Converts

In 1901 Freud embarked on what was to be one of his most famous cases when he undertook the analysis of the patient known, in psychoanalytic literature, as 'Dora'. He also published *The Psychopathology of Everyday Life* which extended his ideas about the role the unconscious mind plays in ordinary events, forcing people into acts of forgetting, slips of the pen and tongue and seemingly insignificant accidents. The following year saw the beginning of the end of Freud's 'splendid isolation' as a thinker. His books had managed to find some sympathetic readers, indeed some who felt that their mental landscape had been transformed by his ideas. At the Wednesday Psychological Society, which was founded this year and began to meet regularly at Berggasse for discussion groups, some of these medical men open to Freud's theories, including Alfred Adler and Wilhelm Stekel, could exchange ideas. The conventional Breuer had long since distanced himself from Freud and his disturbing ideas. Several years before the friendship with Fliess had been severely pressured by an unfortunate occurrence when a patient (originally of Freud's) had nearly died as a result of incompetent surgery by Fliess, compounded by the Berlin doctor's insistence on following his own, misconceived theories about what had gone wrong. The friendship had survived (as had the patient, though more by luck than by Fliess' good management) but now that relationship too was on the wane. He and Fliess were to meet for the last time in Vienna in 1903. Freud was in need of intellectual support and this the Wednesday meetings provided, as well as the agreeable feeling that he was becoming guru to a group of younger, enthusiastic disciples.

Freud, now a full professor at the university and with plenty of private patients, was comfortably off and could afford to travel. He indulged his lifelong interest in the ancient world. He had visited Rome in 1901 and, three years later, he went with his brother Alexander to Athens where the Acropolis made a profound impression on him. Characteristically, in letters in later years, he linked his feelings about the Parthenon with thoughts and memories of his father. Slowly, one small step at a time, psychoanalytic ideas were gaining ground. The Wednesday meetings continued, with new members added to the founding group, and Freud was publishing some of the most significant of his writings to a slightly less hostile academic audience. 1905 saw the appearance of both *Three Essays on the Theory of Sexuality*, Freud's most complete explication so far of his ideas about child sexuality and the instinctual life, and *Jokes and Their Relation to the Unconscious*. Many were scandalised, particularly by the *Three Essays*, but the band of those prepared to listen to Freud's theories with respect and admiration was growing all the time.

His ideas were also making converts outside the narrow circle of Viennese doctors and scientists, almost all Jewish, which had so far provided the members of the Wednesday group. In 1906 Freud received his first letter from the Swiss psychologist Carl Gustav Jung. Jung was in his early thirties and worked at the Burgholzli clinic outside Zurich. Before too many years had passed, Freud and Jung would find their intellectual paths diverging dramatically and the parting of the ways would be exceptionally painful for both men but, in the early days of their relationship, they needed one another. Jung needed the intellectual stimulus that the older man's personality and ideas provided. Freud needed Jung's huge energy, intellect and gift for publicity to push forward the expansion of what was rapidly becoming a psychoanalytical movement. It was also no hindrance that Jung was a non-Jew and a non-Austrian. Psychoanalysis could no longer be dismissed, in anti-Semitic terms, as a strange, probably decadent mishmash of psychology and sexuality dreamt up by a coterie of Viennese Jews.

Freud's first meeting with Jung, in 1907, was a great success and they continued to correspond regularly. Some of the most important members of the early psychoanalytic movement were now in place. Alfred Adler has already been mentioned as one of the founders of the Wednesday Society. In the same year that Jung declared his allegiance by first writing to Freud, Adler introduced Otto Rank to the Wednesday meetings. In 1908 the Budapest doctor Sándor Ferenczi travelled to Vienna and met Freud for the first time. A close friendship was to develop between the two men. Although it was to have its difficult moments, the relationship with Ferenczi was one of the few that did not end in estrangement and mutual recrimination. It lasted until Ferenczi's death in 1933. 1908 also saw the disbandment of the Wednesday Psychological Society and its reconstitution as the Vienna Psychoanalytic Society. Membership continued to grow and meetings now had to be held in a café rather than in Freud's rooms in Berggasse. Many of its members were delegates to the First Congress of Freudian Psychology which took place that same year in Salzburg.

America and the Break with Jung

Psychoanalysis was now ready to step out on to an international stage and the opportunity came in 1909. An invitation arrived at Berggasse from a sympathetic American professor of psychology, Stanley Hall, asking Freud to deliver a series of lectures at Clark University in Worcester, Massachusetts. Freud was not a great lover of America in theory or, as it turned out, in practice. It was, according to him, 'a gigantic mistake.' However, he recognised the significance of this invitation and, together with Jung, now established as crown-prince of the movement, and Ferenczi, he sailed for America in August of that year. Freud may not have liked his time in America but the visit to Worcester was a success. The lectures were attended respectfully, American intellectuals like the legendary Harvard philosopher William James (brother of novelist Henry) wanted to make his acquaintance and, to Freud's slight surprise, there was a small but burgeoning group of would-be psychoanalysts in the States. Freud may have been grumpy about those aspects of America he abhorred but, on his return to Europe, he could congratulate himself on an undoubted triumph. He was on his way to becoming a world figure.

As the psychoanalytic movement expanded (at a conference in Nuremberg in 1910 the International Psychoanalytical Association was founded), so too did the number of its basic writings. Freud continued to publish the results of his own analyses. In 1909 two of his most important case histories appeared – that of the so-called 'Rat Man' and the child-analysis, the only one Freud conducted, called 'Little Hans'. (See the chapter on Case Histories.) The following year he even turned his psychoanalytic eye on an historical figure, publishing *A Childhood Memory of Leonardo Da Vinci*. Later scholarship has revealed devastating flaws in Freud's reasoning (one of his central deductions was based on a mistranslation of a word) but this was to prove one of his own favourites amongst his writings. Years later he described it in a letter as 'the only beautiful thing I have ever written.'

If, as some critics have alleged, Freud had created a kind of secular church in the psychoanalytical movement, then it was destined to have plenty of heresies and schisms and the first rifts began to appear in the years before the First World War. Alfred Adler was an imaginative and original thinker who had been one of the mainstays of the Wednesday meetings since their inauguration but increasingly he found himself in basic disagreement with some key elements in Freud's theories. In 1911 he resigned from the Vienna Psychoanalytic Society. Freud is not seen at his best in these ideological disagreements with fellow analysts. He was unable to see them as genuine intellectual differences and the heretics were swiftly cast into outer darkness. This was the case with Adler. In later years Freud can even be found speculating in private letters on the dubious quality of Adler's sanity. Adler was followed into the realm of non-personhood by Wilhelm Stekel, another founder member of the Wednesday meetings, who resigned from the Vienna Society in 1911.

By far the most serious defection, however, was that of Jung. As mentioned earlier, Jung rapidly became Freud's most favoured disciple. Both men recognised the tensions inherent in their relationship from the beginning. There was so obviously an element of 'father and most favoured son' in it that some kind of eventual break seemed inevitable. When it came, Freud saw it as a break for independence that reflected the unconscious wish to destroy the father and seize his inheritance. Jung, unsurprisingly, like Adler and Stekel before him, saw it as the result of growing intellectual differences between his view of the mind and Freud's. These were honest and genuine differences to Jung, not some masked form of disobedience to a father figure. In late 1912 Jung returned to America to lecture at Fordham University. In theory he was there to expound Freudian ideas but his own beliefs that Freud placed too much emphasis on sexuality in general and the sexual origin of neurosis in particular were clear enough.

Freud did not object to others extending psychoanalytical knowledge but they had to do so from a firm and unwavering conviction in what were (to him) the central realities of the unconscious mind, realities which he had uncovered. Freud was quite explicit about the intellectual dictatorship he imposed. In a pamphlet written soon after Jung's departure from the movement, he wrote, 'Although it is a long time since I was the only psychoanalyst, I consider myself justified in maintaining that even today no one can know better than I do what psychoanalysis is, how it differs from other ways of investigating the life of the mind, and precisely what should be called psychoanalysis and what would be better described by some other name.' It is possible to understand Freud's possessiveness about the movement he had created *ex nihilo* and yet appreciate that, for immensely gifted and original minds like Jung's and Adler's, this kind of intellectual bondage eventually became intolerable. When Jung returned from America, he and Freud did patch up their differences at a meeting in Munich. (The meeting was a dramatic one – at one point during lunch Freud fainted and had to be carried to his hotel room by Jung.) However the parting of the ways was only temporarily postponed. By the end of the year Jung was accusing Freud in letters of causing the rifts in the movement by his insistence on treating all other analysts as children. In 1913 Jung resigned from the editorial committee of Yearbook of Psychoanalysis and by the following year his fundamental disagreements with Freud could no longer be papered over. He resigned from the presidency of the International Psychoanalytical Association.

The break had deep effects on both men, particularly Jung who was about to enter a period of severe, if eventually creative, mental and emotional turmoil during which he occasionally felt he was losing his sanity. However, these squabbles among the psychoanalysts were overshadowed by the outbreak of the First World War. Freud's two sons, Martin and Ernst, were called up for military service in the Austrian army, as were many of the younger members of the International Psychoanalytical Association. Freud himself, at first patriotically in favour of Austria's participation in the war, soon settled into depressed resignation about the follies of mankind as the extent of the carnage and suffering became apparent. 'I do not doubt that mankind will survive even this war,' he wrote, 'but I know for certain that for me and my contemporaries the world will never again be a happy place.' The chief effect of the war on his life was that his earnings plummeted. Analysands in wartime were increasingly difficult to find.

War and Tragedy

In stressful times Freud had always coped by throwing himself into his work and this he did during the war years. With correspondents he may have occasionally been easing himself into the role of an old man ('I have more or less given up work...I believe I have had my time', he wrote to Karl Abraham just before his sixtieth birthday) but the evidence suggests that his mind was as active as ever. One of the last of his case histories, that of the so-called 'Wolf Man', was published towards the end of 1914. He continued to lecture at the University of Vienna, although this lecturing ceased in early 1917. Freud turned instead to preparing lectures for publication, producing two series of *Introductory Lectures on Psychoanalysis*. As the war went on, with no sign of an end to the death and suffering, Freud's thoughts turned to the psychological origin and meaning of mourning. *Mourning and Melancholia* was published. The war also brought home some of the inadequacies of his previous ideas about libido and the life instinct. There could be no clearer evidence of dark, self-destructive forces in the unconscious than what was happening in the trenches and Freud was beginning to believe that, in addition to Eros ('the life instinct'), there must exist what he later called Thanatos ('the death instinct').

There were food shortages in Vienna – and what was almost as important to the cigar-addicted Freud, tobacco shortages. Freud's usual gloomy pessimism about life in general deepened and, as his sixtieth birthday came and went in May 1916, anxieties about his own life ending returned. Freud, grimly rational about most things, had always been superstitiously convinced that the date of his own death was, in some way, written in the stars and he became certain that he would die at the age of sixty two. Despite all these pressures, Freud continued to refine and reassess his ideas on the structure of the mind and how it worked. An unexpected stimulus to his thought came from the arrival in the psychoanalytical movement of a maverick German doctor and therapist, Georg Groddeck. Groddeck was only ten years younger than Freud and had long been critical of psychoanalysis but he had worked it into his own idiosyncratic views on mental health and its treatment. Freud was exceedingly dubious about mystical elements in Groddeck's thinking but he rapidly grew to value him as a correspondent and he thought highly enough of his ideas to appropriate one of Groddeck's terms (the Id) for the new model of the mind he was developing.

When the war finally came to an end, Freud found his finances in severe disarray. His savings had all been in Austrian state bonds which were now virtually worthless. Patients were still few and far between and he could barely scrape a living. Donations to the movement from wealthy sympathisers, like the Hungarian factory owner Anton von Freund, were increasingly welcome. Freund's money was used to establish the International Psychoanalytical Press and Otto Rank, now one of Freud's closest colleagues, was appointed its director. Psychoanalysis itself emerged from the war in a surprisingly flourishing state. Governments were now interested in new ways of treating the hundreds of thousands of severely traumatised soldiers thrown back into civilian life and psychoanalysis proved itself as a therapeutic method. At the 5th International Psychoanalytical Congress, which took place in Budapest six weeks before the armistice was signed, generals and officials from the Austrian and German war ministries mingled with the analysts. Freud was characteristically sceptical about the nature of this sudden governmental interest in his ideas. 'They now think they can use us for practical purposes,' he wrote to one friend, 'but they appear to have no sense of the value of a scientific study of war neuroses.'

In the terribly straitened Austrian economy of the immediate post-war years Freud found most of his patients amongst foreign visitors to Vienna. In 1919 the first American patient appeared at Berggasse and, in the years to come, Freud was to make much of his money from Americans. He was also working on the first draft of what became *Beyond the Pleasure Principle*, in which he attempted to give definitive form to the ideas about 'the death instinct' he had first formulated in the last years of the war. The book was published in 1920. Tragically, in that same year, death intruded into the reality of Freud's world rather than just his ideas. His daughter Sophie died of influenza in Hamburg. Sophie had been his favourite child and Freud was devastated. Sophie had, he wrote, 'been blown away as if she had never been.' Three years later, Sophie's child Heinz, also died, not yet five years old. 'This has killed something in me for good', Freud reported.

Illness and World Fame

In the year of Heinz's death, Freud himself came close to death. He had survived the sixty second year, which he had superstitiously believed would be his last, but in 1923 cancer of the jaw and palate, a consequence of Freud's lifelong passion for cigars, had been diagnosed. He underwent a painful and distressing operation in which the whole of his upper jaw and palate on the right side were removed and a kind of gigantic denture was fitted to isolate his mouth from his nasal cavity. For the rest of his life Freud was to suffer often crippling pain and both his speech and his hearing were affected. More than thirty further operations were required to fight off the encroaching cancer. Freud endured all this with the stoic acceptance of life's vicissitudes which was one of his most admirable qualities.

The year before his cancer was diagnosed Freud had attended the 7th International Psychoanalytical Congress in Berlin and delivered what was to be the last paper he presented to such a gathering. He continued to work, however, and psychoanalysis continued to attract new followers. James and Alix Strachey (brother and sister-in-law of the biographer Lytton) became his official English translators and works by Freud appeared in England under the Hogarth Press imprint of Virginia and Leonard Woolf. Freud's ideas, which had been relatively unknown in Britain, began to be fashionable with Bloomsbury intellectuals and amongst a small group of doctors and psychiatrists. In France, where he was similarly unrecognised, his most vociferous followers appeared in the surprising guise of the avant-garde poets and writers soon to be known as Surrealists. During the war André Breton, a young poet later to be christened the 'Pope of Surrealism' (he was to prove even more intolerant of intellectual disagreement than Freud), had come across psychoanalysis during his work with shell-shocked soldiers. In 1921 he visited Freud in Vienna and returned to Paris full of the wonders of this man who 'seemed to have turned the world of the spirit upside down.' In 1923 the first biography of Freud was published, written by Fritz Wittels. Predictably, Freud was unimpressed. 'Of course, I would never have wished for or promoted such a book', he wrote to Wittels, adding, 'You know too little about your subject and can consequently not avoid the danger of doing violence to him through your analytical efforts.'

By the mid-1920s Freud was a famous figure both in Vienna and the wider world. In 1924 he was awarded the Freedom of the City of Vienna. Ever the pessimist he succeeded, in a letter to Karl Abraham, in linking this honour with his perennial death-anxiety. 'The idea that my 68th birthday the day after tomorrow could be my last,' he wrote, 'must have occurred to others too since the city of Vienna hastened to award me the Freedom of the City for which one usually waits until one's 70th birthday.' Across in the United States, Freud was now sufficiently well-known that, at the time of the sensational Leopold-Loeb murder trial, a Chicago newspaper offered him $25,000 to analyse the two defendants from afar. Freud refused.

A Collected Edition of Freud's works had long been suggested and, in 1925, the first volumes were published. Yet psychoanalysis could still evoke controversy and suspicion. Using a law against quack doctors, the Vienna Medical Society had started legal proceedings against Theodor Reik, a well-known analyst who happened not to be medically trained. Freud, who thought well of Reik and always believed that 'psychoanalysis, whether as a science or as a technique, is not a purely medical matter', was angered by the eventual decision to bar him from practising. He wrote a vigorous defence of 'lay' analysis that was published in 1926 but, more and more (particularly in the US), psychoanalysis became exclusively the preserve of the medically trained.

The Last Years

Freud's life, as well as his life's work, was more and more in the hands of the medical profession. Operation followed operation in an attempt to stave off the effects of his oral cancer and relieve the suffering it caused. On a number of occasions he travelled to Berlin for treatment at the Tegel sanatorium. In 1930 a heart attack finally forced him to give up smoking. In the autumn of that same year his mother died at the age of 95, having seen her belief in her eldest son's genius more than fulfilled. Freud wrote to Ferenczi, 'It has had a curious effect on me, this great event. No pain, no mourning, which can probably be explained by the accompanying circumstances of her great age and by compassion for her helplessness at the end, and together with that a feeling of liberation, of being freed that I think I also understand. I could not die as long as she was alive, and now I can. Somehow at the deeper levels life's values have noticeably altered.'

As always, Freud continued to work. Since at least 1913 and the publication of *Totem and Taboo* he had been using the insights of psychoanalysis not only to examine the workings of the mind but to pursue larger ideas about the origins of society and civilisation. *The Future of an Illusion*, published in 1928, encapsulated his ideas about religion. Freud, who always prided himself on his rationalism and his faith in the power of science, had little or no time for any religion and the book is a withering, reductive examination of the psychology behind religious belief. *Civilisation and Its Discontents* (1930) provided a summation of Freud's thinking about the conflict between the individual's instinctual needs and the social mores which necessarily constrain them.

The book's origins lay in Freud's responses to the barbarity and suffering of the First World War. By the early thirties a new barbarity was beginning to show itself. Freud had always been aware of the anti-Semitism that lurked in the shadows of the European mind, occasionally daring to show itself. It was often impossible not to be aware of it. From 1897 to 1910 the mayor of Vienna was Karl Lueger who was openly and blatantly anti-Semitic. In an interview conducted in the 1920s Freud had told his interviewer, 'I speak the German language and I live in the world of German culture. Spiritually I felt myself to be a German until I was able to observe the growth of anti-Semitism in Germany and Austria. Since then I have preferred to feel myself a Jew.' Even Freud, the deepest of pessimists, could have had no idea at the time the effects that anti-Semitism was to have on German culture, his fellow-Jews and on his own family.

When the Nazis came to power in 1933 and the book-burnings began, Freud's works were amongst those thrown into the bonfires. Soon many German-Jewish analysts were forced into exile by the new regime. For the time Freud, in Vienna, remained secure. He was a figure of world renown. On his eightieth birthday, May 6th 1936, congratulations arrived at Berggasse from well-wishers as different, but as distinguished, as Einstein and Virginia Woolf, James Joyce and Albert Schweitzer. Two years later the Austrian Chancellor Schusnigg was forced to resign, Austria was annexed to the German Reich on the 13th March 1938 and Hitler marched in triumph into Vienna, the city where he had been little more than a vagrant twenty five years earlier.

Immediately there was a wave of anti-Semitic persecution in the city. Freud and his family were saved from the worst humiliations by his reputation but the apartment in Berggasse was searched and Freud's daughter Anna spent a day in the custody of the Gestapo. It was time for him to leave the city in which he had spent nearly eighty years. Again, because of his stature as a world-famous thinker, Freud was luckier than most of Vienna's Jews. Despite his own stubborn reluctance to leave, and the attempts by the Nazis to keep him in the city, exit visas were obtained for the Freud family. He left Vienna on the 4th June and two days later arrived in London.

Freud was, by this time, an old and very sick man. The family moved into 20, Maresfield Gardens in Hampstead where, despite his illness, he worked on his last book, *Moses and Monotheism*. His cancer was now inoperable. In early August of the following year he finally gave up his practice. Anna and his friend and doctor Max Schur nursed him through last days of terrible pain and distress. In the early hours of September 23rd 1939, Freud lapsed into a coma and died.

Chapter Two: Freud's Ideas

Freud was writing, thinking and developing the ideas for which he is famous over a period of more than fifty years. Inevitably, in a thinker of his imagination and originality, the ideas did not remain static over those decades and, equally inevitably, contradictions can be found in his voluminous writings. Some critics have used these contradictions as a rod with which to beat Freud's back. He would have been contemptuous of the notion that a scientist (such as he always held himself to be) could not change his ideas on the basis of new evidence and it is difficult not to agree that such critics are wasting their energies. Yes, there are contradictions in Freud's writings but they are insignificant compared to the broad unfolding of his thought over his working life. In order to get some sense of what his ideas were, it is possible to divide them into four, very general categories. In even more general terms it is possible to say that, at different times of his life, Freud was more concerned with one of these four categories rather than the others. From the late 1880s to the early 1900s, he was exploring the ideas of the conscious and unconscious mind which emerged from his practice with his patients. In parallel with this, from the mid 1890s to the years just before the outbreak of the First World War, he formulated his ideas about sexual development from childhood to puberty and beyond. As early as the 1890s Freud attempted to fashion some general theory of the structure of the mind into which he could fit his new ideas but it was only during the First World War and the early 1920s that he laid out the tripartite division into id, ego and superego that represents his most elaborate thinking on the subject. In the last decade and a half of his life his most notable writings were concerned with what psychoanalysis could say about broader issues of culture and society.

The Conscious and the Unconscious Mind

Freud was not the first person to write of the unconscious mind. The notion that there are mental processes, which effect our behaviour but which are not accessible to the conscious, rational mind, is present in an assortment of texts dating back to classical times. However, no one before Freud had made a systematic study of the idea and certainly no one before Freud had dared to suggest that mental processes were, very largely, unconscious and that the conscious, rational mind was only the tip of an iceberg, a small island of self-awareness in the great ocean of the unconscious. He was drawn to this belief by what gradually unfolded as he treated his hysteric and neurotic patients in the 1890s and also by what was revealed as he passed through a period of intense introspection and self-analysis, particularly in the aftermath of the death of his father in 1896.

With patients hypnotism had initially worked, as in Breuer's case of Anna O, to bring repressed memories to the surface. In the early 1890s Freud used 'the pressure technique' to coax his patients towards accessing material that they had repressed. As they lay on his soon-to-be famous couch in Berggasse 19, he pressed his hand on their foreheads and simply asked them questions, encouraging them to slip past the censorship imposed by the rational mind. Finally he adopted the technique of 'free association'. Sitting out of sight of the patients and saying as little as was necessary to keep them talking, Freud allowed them to reveal whatever was going through their minds without the fear of judgement, condemnation or ridicule. One thought led to another and the process took Freud and his patients in some surprising directions. The material that emerged from these sessions provided the foundations for Freud's ideas about sexual development (see below) and the division between the conscious and the unconscious. The unconscious was the result of repression and what were repressed were all those thoughts, desires and feelings which the conscious self found unacceptable. The minds of Freud's patients were divided minds. There was the part (the conscious) which was aware of its own thoughts and desires. And there was the much larger part revealed by free association (the unconscious) which was a storeroom, difficult of access, where patients kept all their dark and transgressive thoughts and desires.

Why were so many of his patients' thoughts and desires unacceptable to them? Freud put forward the idea of two opposing principles that lay behind behaviour. The 'pleasure principle' is what governs us at birth and this principle pushes us towards the instant gratification of all our wishes. As we grow up and discover that we have to live with, and adapt to, the natural world and other people, the 'reality principle' comes into operation. Deferment of gratification is seen to be a necessity. In particular our sexual drive, what Freud called 'the libido', that unruly drive which he saw as the main motive for most behaviour, has to be re-directed into socially acceptable channels. Mental health, according to Freud, was dependent on how successful people were in re-directing libido into socially acceptable behaviour. His neurotic and hysteric patients had failed to find successful means of re-directing libido. The conflict between their pleasure principle and their reality principle was unresolved and the result was their illness. Only by accessing the repressed material in their unconscious minds and working through it could a resolution of the conflict be reached and the mental illness overcome. Then, in Freud's gloomily modest assessment, neurotic misery could be turned into ordinary human unhappiness.

But, of course, the conflict between conscious and unconscious was not restricted to the hysterical and the neurotic. What Freud was proposing was not just an outline of the 'sick' mind but also a general structure of the human mind. It was simply that the neuroses provided ideal opportunities for a scientist such as himself to glimpse this general structure at work. There were other signposts to the division between conscious and unconscious. Most importantly there were dreams.

Dreams had long fascinated Freud. There are references to them and to ideas about them in his letters as a student. In the early 1890s, as he began to treat his patients with the revolutionary new therapy that he had not yet named 'psychoanalysis' and to make use of free association on a regular basis, he was struck by the frequency with which they referred to their dreams. Dreams, occurring when we are asleep and the conscious apparatus of censorship and repression are least vigilant, seemed to Freud a rich potential source of material to support his developing theories of the unconscious. At the same time he was himself going through a painful period of introspection and self-analysis which came to a crisis-point with the death of his father Jacob in 1896. During this time he subjected his own dreams to careful scrutiny. (A number of the dreams discussed in *The Interpretation of Dreams* are Freud's own, although he doesn't identify them as such in the book.) One complex dream, known as the dream of 'Irma's injection', which he dreamed while staying at the Schloss Bellevue outside Vienna in 1895, came to seem of central importance to his dream-theory when he recognised it as the fulfilment of an unconscious wish. (In a letter to Fliess five years later, Freud jokingly speculated about the possibility of a plaque on the wall of the Schloss marking the site where the secret of dreams was revealed to him. Some forty years after his death this became a reality when such a plaque was indeed placed on the Schloss Bellevue.)

Freud's central ideas about dreams are embodied in one of his most famous books, *The Interpretation of Dreams* (see Chapter Three). Essentially they spring from that one central insight that dreams act as wish-fulfilments.

Freud also found evidence of the unconscious in operation in two commonplace phenomena – jokes and human mistakes. Two of his most fascinating books, *The Psychopathology of Everyday Life* and *Jokes and their Relation to the Unconscious* (see Chapter Three), record his thoughts on these subjects. The rather daunting title of *The Psychopathology of Everyday Life* disguises the fact that the book is largely about one of the psychoanalytic ideas most familiar to the average person – the so-called Freudian slip. In Freud's view of the bipartite division of the mind into conscious and unconscious, it is as if the unruly thoughts and desires of the latter are always seeking means of expression, bubbling away beneath the surface of the conscious and looking for an outlet. Freud contends that apparently meaningless mistakes – slips of the pen and tongue, acts of omission and forgetting – carry hidden messages from the unconscious. One example which he gives from his own experience is telling in its simplicity. Freud had run out of blotting paper yet, day after day, forgot to go to the shop and buy some more. The reason, he finally concluded, was that one of the German words for blotting paper is 'fliesspapier'. This was the time of his painful falling out with his friend Wilhelm Fliess and he did not want to be reminded of this. So he repeatedly forgot to go and buy 'fliesspapier.' Not all Freud's examples are as simple or as convincing as this (indeed some are enormously convoluted and remarkably unconvincing) but the very popularity of the term 'Freudian slip' indicates that he had highlighted a phenomenon common to everyone and given it a plausible explanation. Many, although not all, Freudian slips obviously do represent intrusions of unconscious thought processes into consciousness.

Similarly Freud's contention that jokes, far from just being innocent vehicles of comedy, are also freighted with unconscious loves and fears and hatreds coincides with most people's experience of ordinary life. Of course, some jokes are innocent enough and Freud himself acknowledged (initially, at least) that wordplay and verbal dexterity carried little baggage from the unconscious. But many jokes deal with subjects – sexuality, ethnicity, family relationships – that arouse strong feelings. Freud argued that the tensions created by these subjects, denied expression in socially unacceptable behaviour, found release in the socially acceptable form of jokes. Many jokes, like Freudian slips, were examples of the unconscious working its way into the conscious.

In all of these phenomena – the behaviour of his neurotic patients, dreams, Freudian slips, jokes – Freud found evidence for his ideas about the conscious and unconscious mind, for his central argument that much of mental life was unconscious and that only certain individual acts and thoughts were the result of consciousness and rationality.

Sexuality and Sexual Development

In addition to his assertion of the power of the irrational unconscious over our reason, Freud's other great and controversial blow to the self-esteem of the late nineteenth century world stemmed from his insistence on the centrality of sexual instincts, of the libido. Not only did he argue that his work with his patients showed that neuroses and hysteria had their origins in sexual desires and impulses but he claimed that the sexual instinct was present in children. And not just in children who grew up to become mentally ill but in all children.

Essentially what Freud wanted to do was extend the narrow definition of 'sexuality' prevalent in medical circles at the end of the nineteenth century. To most doctors at the time, sexuality referred to genital contact and intercourse between adults of different sex. In a range of writings, but most particularly in *Three Essays on Sexuality* of 1905, Freud pointed out how much of human behaviour this excluded. There were those – Freud called them inverts – who were attracted, either at all times or for periods of their sexual lives, to the same sex. There were those – Freud called them perverts – whose libidos were directed towards other parts of the body. There were fetishists whose libidos were directed towards inanimate objects, because of early experiences which had created a symbolic link between the object and the sex drive. There were those (sadists and masochists) whose wish was either to inflict or receive pain during sexual activity. Sadism, according to Freud, had its roots in the aggression that was a part of the sexual drive, particularly the male sexual drive. Masochism was sadism which had turned in upon the self. And, finally, there was the most taboo area of all – the childhood sexuality which Freud had uncovered in his patients during the new method of treatment he called psychoanalysis. Today some of Freud's terminology may seem quaint, even offensive. Some of the sexual activities he characterised as 'perversions' (oral and anal sex, for example) might seem perfectly normal. The important point is that Freud was insisting that definitions of sexuality at the time needed to be broadened if any true understanding of the subject was to be reached. He brought whole areas of human behaviour out of the darkness in which contemporary thought placed them and demanded that they be given proper scientific attention.

Freud's ideas about childhood sexuality caused most furore at the time. He was not unprepared for this. Indeed he had an explanation for why this should be the case. There was a special process of infantile amnesia that, between the ages of six and eight, operated to repress early sexual thoughts and any attempts to overcome this repressive amnesia would necessarily meet strong resistance. However, Freud was insistent that sexual impulses were present in the child from a very early age and that there were, in fact, several stages of infantile sexual development. Between the ages of six and eight these early sexual activities and thoughts entered what Freud called the 'latency period', only re-emerging in puberty.

In his writings of the first decade of the twentieth century, Freud gradually built up his ideas about the stages of infantile sexual development. Each stage is characterised by the particular ways in which the child gains sexual pleasure. The first stage is the 'oral stage' in which the emphasis is, as the name makes clear, on the mouth. Sucking – of the mother's breast, of the thumb – is of paramount importance. The breast, as the source of food, becomes also the source of pleasure and the child focuses strong feelings of love and hate upon it. Withholding of the breast is equivalent to the withholding of love. The second stage is the 'anal stage' which occurs between the ages of one and three and centres on the learning of voluntary control of the bladder and the bowels. Both producing and withholding stools becomes a source of pleasure to the child and the cause of praise or blame by parents and carers. The third stage is the 'phallic stage' and lasts from about the ages of three to five. Sensual pleasure is now focussed on the genitals, stimulated first by everyday activities like washing or urinating and then deliberately by the child itself. It is at this stage that sexual difference is discovered. Transition from stage to stage in this development is not easy and it is only too possible to become 'fixated' at any given stage, with consequences ongoing into adulthood. Those fixated at the 'oral' stage, for example, continue to give over-emphasis to the mouth. Smoking and excessive drinking or eating are signs of those stuck at this stage. Those fixated at the 'anal' stage can become retentive individuals (obsessively tidy, demanding of order) or expulsive (recklessly untidy, anti-social).

The three stages of oral, anal and phallic lead on to the final challenge facing the individual child – overcoming the demands of what Freud called the Oedipus complex. First glimpsed in the experiences, thoughts and dreams conveyed to him by his patients, the idea of the Oedipus complex as a universal human experience emerged from the painful self-analysis Freud conducted in the mid-1890s, after the death of his father. Recognising in himself the same hidden desires that his patients were revealing, Freud decided that everybody shared this rite of passage.

The story of Oedipus comes from Greek mythology. King Laius of Thebes and his wife Jocasta are about to become parents when it is foretold that the child will grow up to murder his father and marry his mother. Anxious to avoid this undesirable future, Laius arranges for his new-born son to be left on a mountainside to die. Shepherds take pity on the child and rescue him. Eventually the boy is brought up by the king and queen of Corinth and named Oedipus. Ignorant of his true identity, Oedipus, as a young man, leaves Corinth when the Delphic Oracle repeats the prediction about killing his father and marrying his mother. On the road to Thebes he meets Laius by chance, they quarrel and Oedipus ends by killing the man he does not realise is his own father. Travelling onwards he defeats the Sphinx, which has been troubling the city, by correctly deciphering her riddle. Made the new king of Thebes, he marries the widow of the old king, his own mother Jocasta. When the truth finally emerges Oedipus blinds himself and Jocasta hangs herself. The reason that this myth has such resonance, according to Freud, is that it dramatises the three-way love triangle that exists in everyone's early childhood. The child falls in love with the mother, longs for total possession of her, becomes frantically jealous of the father and fantasises about killing him so that the mother is the child's alone.

Resolution of the Oedipus complex is essential for healthy sexual development. The way forward is different for boys and for girls. A boy, murderously jealous of his father's possession of his mother, is none the less aware of the power of his father. He fantasises that his father knows of his desires and will punish him by castrating him. Only by abandoning his desire for his mother as a sexual object can he avoid this terrible fate and move on. For a girl, the way forward is even more difficult. She also desires her mother and fears the response of her father. But she discovers that she is already castrated – she lacks a penis. She suffers not castration anxiety but penis envy. She turns away from her mother towards the possessor of the envied penis – her father. Today many of the details of Freud's Oedipus complex, particularly its phallocentric explanation of female development, may seem absurd. But this stems largely from Freud's wish to create an all-encompassing story to explain sexual development. Much of what he was the first to explicitly acknowledge and attempt to explain is clearly true. Boys do form intense relationships with their mothers and do resent their fathers. Girls do so with their fathers. Boys (and men) do suffer anxiety about their penises and possible castration. The Oedipus complex is not the entirely self-sufficient explanation Freud believed but it is clear that it does, in part, reflect genuine human emotions and fantasies.

For Freud, the Oedipal stage is followed by the latency period, the years in which sexual activity is dormant and the memories of earlier sexual feelings are repressed by infantile amnesia. Sexuality only emerges again in adolescence when the time is right for the 'genital' stage, the direction of sexual feelings towards intercourse with an adult of the opposite sex. Successful attainment of this sexual satisfaction is the end result of the long period of development, beginning with the oral pleasures of the breast, which he had identified. To Freud, this psychosexual development was inseparable from social and emotional development. It is his insistence on this interlinking of sexual, social and personal maturation, and the potential hurdles facing the individual as he or she works to achieve it, that marked his work at a time when few others were prepared even to acknowledge it.

The Structure of the Mind

Freud's original division of the mind was bipartite – into the conscious and the unconscious. The unconscious was the material repressed because it was unacceptable to the conscious. Over the years Freud came to recognise the shortcomings of this simple model and, by the early 1920s, he had arrived at a view which extended this to a tripartite structure. With some small modifications, this was to remain Freud's model of how the mind worked until the end of his life. The three parts of the mind in his model, he named the ego, the id and the superego.

The oldest and most primitive part of the mind is the id. Taken from the Latin word for 'it', it was a term Freud borrowed from the maverick Viennese psychologist and philosopher Georg Groddeck. The id is the mind we are all born with, a seething mass of wholly selfish desires and the impulses aimed at the immediate and complete gratification of those desires. It is the id which is the driving force behind what Freud called the pleasure principle. As we develop and grow older we must leave the id behind, curb its insistent demands and make them conform to the real world and the other people in it. But we never do really leave the id behind. Its demands may be repressed but they remain, expressing themselves in phenomena as different as dreams, neurotic symptoms and Freudian slips. In most respects the id plays the same role in Freud's later model of the mind as the unconscious does in his earlier one.

The ego is the rational part of the mind, the part that reacts to the outside world and allows the individual to adapt to reality, to acknowledge the 'reality principle.' The ego (the word is Latin for 'I') develops from the id but comes to exercise control over it. The ego provides the individual with the sense of self and watches over the instinctual demands of the id, deciding whether, when and how they can be gratified. In most respects the ego plays the role the conscious played in Freud's initial bipartite model, although Freud made clear that some of the monitoring and censoring of the id that the ego carries out is done unconsciously. Freud's most telling analogy of the relationship between the id and the ego is to compare it with the relationship of a horse and its rider. Occasionally, of course, a horse will slip from its rider's control, just as the instinctual demands of the id occasionally elude the restraints of ego, but, mostly, the horse is guided and controlled by its rider.

The third component of Freud's most developed model of the mind's structure is what he called the super-ego. The origins of this new concept of the superego lay in Freud's thinking on narcissism. In papers published during the First World War and later, he had created his own definition of what he called 'primary narcissism', a period of child development when all libido was directed, not outwards to others, but solely towards the self. This megalomaniac self-centredness is characteristic of the very small baby who believes him or herself to be the centre of the universe. As the child develops and learns to adapt to the real world and to others, in other words as the ego develops, another part of the mind is created which monitors the ego in much the same way that the ego supervises the id. This super-ego demands perfection of the ego, that it meet impossible ideals of thought and behaviour. In essence, the super-ego is the internalised voice of parents, carers and society which provide the individual with the rules and regulations that guide it when it moves beyond primary narcissism. Often operating unconsciously, the super-ego provides us all with our conscience, our sense of what is right and what is wrong, and demands that we often behave in ways acceptable to society at large rather than to our own individual urges.

In a mature, mentally healthy individual the id, ego and super-ego interact in a balanced way. In all of us, however, the three components of the mind can create anxiety and guilt. Real, potentially threatening events perceived by the ego can be anxiety-provoking. The nagging conscience of the super-ego causes anxiety when we fall short of its demands. And, of course, the thwarted instinctual demands of the id can create an unfocussed, neurotic anxiety, the origins of which are not immediately accessible to the conscious.

Culture and Society

Freud was not a narrowly specialist scientist. He was a man deeply immersed in the wider culture of the Austro-Hungarian Empire and Western Europe. Although not fond of music (with the exception of opera), his interest in and knowledge of the other arts was considerable. He was well read in both classic and modern literature and had a deep love for the visual arts, especially sculpture. When he could afford to do so, he built up a considerable collection of *objets d'art*, particularly antique statuettes. (Much of the collection can still be seen at the Freud Museum in Hampstead.)

Freud soon came to believe that art and his newly discovered psychoanalysis had much to offer one another and, as early as 1907, he wrote a paper on the part played by dreams and delusions in a now-forgotten novel, *Gradiva* by the German writer Wilhelm Jensen. In Jensen's story of a young archaeologist who becomes obsessed by the girl in an antique relief (to the detriment of his relationships in real life) Freud saw evidence that the writer had shown ideas about repression and anxiety in action similar to his own. Jensen's emphasis on the dreams of his protagonist was further proof that artists could instinctively reach truths about mental life that the scientist could attain only by careful analysis of data.

Freud wrote papers on other artists – Michelangelo, Dostoevsky – but his most considerable work analysing the psyche of artistic genius was his study of Leonardo Da Vinci. This essay has been much criticised and Freud laid himself open to later attack by inadvertently using a mistranslation of Leonardo's writings. At the core of Freud's interpretation of Leonardo's psychosexual make-up is a description by the artist of one of his earliest childhood memories. While he was in his cradle, Leonardo said, a vulture came down from the skies, opened his mouth with its tail and struck him many times on the lips. Faced with this unlikely memory, Freud interprets it as a fantasy and links it with Leonardo's presumed homosexuality, the bird's tail being a symbol for the penis. He then uses his extensive knowledge of mythology to make further points based on the mythological role of the vulture in Ancient Egypt. Unfortunately, the bird Leonardo describes is a kite not a vulture. All of these further points are invalidated. However, assuming that one places trust in the idea of Freudian symbols, the notion that the childhood memory is a fantasy disguising an expression of passive homosexuality remains sustainable. And many of Freud's further arguments, from the general contention that Leonardo's astonishing creativity had its roots in the sublimation of his sexuality to specific points about individual paintings, are imaginative and thought-provoking.

Freud's willingness to apply psychoanalytic theory to discussion of the arts shows how his ambitions for his ideas grew. Initially, he was working to explain the behaviour of neurotic and hysteric patients. Then he was working to apply what he had learned from his patients to a general theory of the human mind. By the time he wrote his most significant works on culture, religion and society (in

41

the last two decades of his life) he was prepared to argue that almost any human behaviour could be explained by reference to psychoanalytic theory. It could even explain the beginnings of civilisation and the true significance of religious faith.

To the perennially pessimistic Freud, civilisation was a mixed blessing. Civilised society provides us with obvious benefits. It provides defence against the often violent indifference of nature to our fate. It secures our relationships with one another and protects us against the unfettered expression of the instinctual desires of others. It gives us our greatest achievements in the arts and sciences. Yet it comes at a major cost. It demands the repression of our most basic urges. In order to conform to society, and to live with other people, the needs of the id, our most fundamental urges to selfish pleasure and satisfaction, have, to a large extent, to be repressed or channelled in new directions. Civilisation and civilised behaviour necessarily involves individual unhappiness.

Over the millennia people have devised ways of assuaging and explaining the unhappiness inherent in civilisation. Most important of these has been religion. In his later works on religion and society, most particularly *The Future of an Illusion*, Freud explains what he believes psychoanalysis can tell us about religious belief. Although he acknowledges the importance of religion as a means by which men could be persuaded to renounce fulfilment of their instinctual wishes, and although (ever the intellectual elitist) he considers that all but a few would never have agreed to the renunciation of instinct that civilisation demands without religion, Freud's lack of sympathy with religious ideas is clear. Religion is compared to neurosis, something to be overcome if full maturity is to be achieved. Religious practices have the same psychological roots as the rituals of obsessional neurotics. Belief in gods, and religious ideas generally, spring from man's helplessness in the face of nature. Just as the helpless child turns for protection to the father, religious believers turn to father figures that have been created for them by earlier generations in the shape of the gods. For Freud the future lay not with religion but with science.

Chapter Three: Freud's Major Works

Studies on Hysteria (1895)

'Hysterics suffer mainly from reminiscences.'

Studies on Hysteria, written in collaboration with Josef Breuer and published in 1895, was the book in which Freud's ideas about psychoanalysis, a term he coined the following year, first began to come together. The book is divided between theoretical chapters and descriptions of particular case histories, the material on which the theory is based. Of the case histories, the most significant is that of Breuer's patient Anna O. (see Chapter Four). The other cases are Freud's and they are all women whose hysterical symptoms can be traced to traumatic events which have remained psychically unresolved. Freud and Breuer make the claim that individual hysterical symptoms disappear when the events that provoked them are brought into the open and thoroughly described by the patients themselves. This is what Anna O. called her 'talking cure.' The theoretical chapters of the book, for a reader familiar with the later history of the two authors' relationship, are notable for a marked tension between a desire (Breuer's) not to stray too far outside the boundaries of conventional wisdom and an ambition (Freud's) to make new and adventurous claims. It was Freud's insistence that the precipitating traumas in hysterical patients were exclusively sexual that was to cause a serious rift between himself and Breuer in the period after the publication of *Studies on Hysteria*.

The Interpretation of Dreams (1899/1900)

'The interpretation of dreams is in fact the royal road to a knowledge of the unconscious; it is the securest foundation of psychoanalysis...'

The Interpretation of Dreams was first published at the end of 1899 but, in a move that now seems an appropriate hint that the book would be of great importance to the new century, the publishers dated it 1900. Yet few books of such importance have been greeted with such indifference when first published. In two years *The Interpretation of Dreams* sold just over 350 copies. It took eight years for the initial print-run of 600 to sell out. The central contention of Freud's book is that dreams are the consequences of a battle between the conscious and the unconscious. The unconscious teems with thoughts, desires and wishes that look for expression but, in ordinary, waking life, the conscious mind represses these. In dreams, the unconscious partially evades the censorship imposed upon it and its wishes and desires achieve fulfilment. However, because the wishes and desires (largely sexual and related to the longings of infantile sexuality) have such power to disturb the individual, even in dreams they are fulfilled only in disguised form. There is the manifest dream, the dream the dreamer remembers and recounts, and the latent dream, the hidden material behind the manifest dream. Freud described what he called 'the dream-work' by which the mind disguises the material that is seeking expression and hides the latent dream behind the manifest dream. Dream-work makes use of a number of different techniques. There is condensation, in which one idea or image stands for a sequence of interconnected ideas or images. There is displacement, in which a strong and troubling emotion is detached from its real source and 'displaced' onto another, often trivial idea or image. Freud identified a number of other techniques of disguise, including (most famously) symbolisation in which a range of neutral objects in dreams stand in for the male and female sexual organs and for sexual activity. (Ironically, given the fact that Freudian symbolism has become so well-known an idea, Freud paid the subject little attention in *The Interpretation of Dreams*. It is only in later works that he creates a list of potential Freudian symbols that includes a bewilderingly large array of objects from watering cans and pistols to bottle and pockets.) For Freud the task of the psychoanalyst was to use methods like free association to reach the latent dream hidden behind the manifest dream just as it was to get beyond the neurotic symptoms to the unacknowledged desires that had created them. And, since everyone, both neurotic and non-neurotic, dreamed, his theory of dreams was clear evidence that psychoanalysis had moved beyond the treatment of the mentally distressed and was now a general theory of the human mind, applicable to all. Throughout the rest of his life, Freud continued to think that *The Interpretation of Dreams* was his most significant book. 'Insight such as this falls to one's lot but once in a lifetime,' he wrote in a foreword to a 1931 edition of it. Much of Freud's thinking about dreams has been overtaken by the progress of scientific research, as Freud's harshest critics have been quick to point out. Yet they forget that it was Freud who was the first to reinstate dreams as a worthy subject for scientific scrutiny. Without Freud and *The Interpretation of Dreams*, much of the later research used to discredit his theories would not have existed. Often the fate of the pioneer is to be attacked by later generations for whom he or she has opened new fields of study and it is a fate that Freud has suffered more than most.

The Psychopathology of Everyday Life (1901)

It is in *The Psychopathology of Everyday Life* that Freud most extensively discusses parapraxes or what we now, quite routinely, refer to as Freudian slips. He first mentions parapraxis in a letter to Fliess in August 1898 and it is through parapraxes, as well as through dreams, that Freud was able to extend the discoveries that he had made working with the neurotically disturbed to the mental life of everyone, neurotic or not. Freud's central contention in the book is that events and actions that we dismiss as trivial, meaningless accidents and mistakes carry hidden meanings which reveal the unconscious workings of the mind. From the forgetting of names and foreign words, through mistakes in speech and writing to actions carried out in error, these parapraxes can be analysed and the unconscious motivations behind them unveiled.

Three Essays on the Theory of Sexuality (1905)

These essays, which summarise Freud's thinking at the time on the subject of sexuality, are amongst his most significant and ground-breaking works. Work with his patients had revealed to Freud how limited was the definition of 'sexuality' prevalent in medical circles at the end of the nineteenth century. In the *Three Essays* he wanted to show how much of human behaviour the conventional definition excluded. There were those – Freud called them inverts – who were attracted, either at all times or for periods of their sexual lives, to the same sex. There were those – Freud called them perverts – whose libidos were directed towards other parts of the body. There were fetishists whose libidos were directed towards inanimate objects, because of early experiences which had created a symbolic link between the object and the sex drive. There were those (sadists and masochists) whose wish was either to inflict or receive pain during sexual activity. And, finally, there was the most taboo area of all – the childhood sexuality which Freud had uncovered in his patients during the new method of treatment he called psychoanalysis. Today some of Freud's terminology may seem quaint, even offensive. Some of the sexual activities he characterised as 'perversions' (oral and anal sex, for example) might seem perfectly normal. The important point is that Freud was insisting that definitions of sexuality at the time needed to be broadened if any true understanding of the subject was to be reached. In *Three Essays on Sexuality* he brought whole areas of human behaviour out of the darkness in which contemporary thought placed them and demanded that they be given proper scientific attention.

Jokes and their Relation to
the Unconscious (1905)

When Wilhelm Fliess read the proofs of *The Interpretation of Dreams*, he remarked to Freud that many of the dreams recorded in it were full of jokes and plays on words. This comment chimed both with Freud's own interest, already established, in the psychology behind joking and what we find funny, and his own observation that jokes employed many of the strategies (condensation and displacement, for example) which he had identified in dreams. *Jokes and their Relation to the Unconscious* is the ultimate result of Freud's explorations of the parallels. Freud saw more than just parallels, however, between the strategies of dream work and the techniques employed in the telling of successful jokes. Some jokes, he argued, served the same purpose as some dreams in allowing socially or personally unacceptable material from the unconscious to emerge in disguised form. Freud divided dreams into two categories. 'Innocent' jokes depended on wordplay and verbal dexterity. They resorted to little in the way of disguise and Freud clearly thought, at this stage, that they had nothing to tell about the unconscious mind. (In later writings he was to change his mind and decide that even 'innocent' jokes were not so innocent after all.) 'Tendentious' jokes are those which disguise aggression or libido. By a circuitous route, these allow the satisfaction of an instinct despite the obstacles that social and personal mores put in the way. An example (although not one Freud used himself) would be the mother-in-law joke of English music-hall tradition. Very strong feeling and resentful misogyny lodged in the unconscious are given an outlet through the telling of a disparaging story that is none the less allowable because it is 'only a joke.' *Jokes and their Relation to the Unconscious* is not one of Freud's easiest books to read. Jokes get easily lost in translation, either from one language to another or across the passage of time, and analyses of the nature of humour are rarely very enjoyable works themselves. However, it is an important book in Freud's career in that it showed, like *The Psychopathology of Everyday Life*,

47

that he was interested in taking the insights and methods of psycho-analysis and applying them not just to neurotic symptoms and to therapy but to the creation of a comprehensive view of the human mind.

Totem and Taboo (1913)

Totem and Taboo is the first major work in which Freud attempted to use psychoanalysis to throw light on wider cultural, anthropological and religious questions. It is the book in which his controversial ideas about the primal horde, the killing of the primal father and the role played by the Oedipus complex in the origins of religion and of many cultural and social institutions are first aired. The ideas are ingenious ones although today few anthropologists would see them as having any basis in historical fact. Even as Freud describes his theory, it seems more to carry the force of myth than of reality. It is hard to tell how far Freud intended his description to be taken as an historical account.

Plenty of scientists at the time believed that early man would have lived, like apes, in groups dominated by a single powerful male. This alpha male would have monopolised the females of the group and forced the younger males to look outside the group for mates. Freud took these ideas an imaginative stage further. He envisaged a scenario in which the younger males, weary of the father's dominance and monopoly of the females, joined forces to kill him and take possession of the women. Overcome by guilt at this act of parricide, they needed to find a means of expiation. From their act derived the notions of totem and taboo. The totem was the representative of the murdered father, an animal given special privileges throughout the year but ritually sacrificed and eaten on one day in the year as a reminder of the act of liberation that the killing had been. The taboo against incest was instituted to prevent further internecine warfare and competition for the women. The dreadful act of parricide would be avoided in future by ensuring that the circumstances in which it had taken place could not recur. Over time these reminders of a past collective guilt would be institutionalised as religious mysteries.

These may be the most striking passages in the book, and they are the ones that attracted and continue to attract most attention, but they actually take up only part of one essay out of the four that make up *Totem and Taboo*. The earlier essays discuss other elements of 'primitive' religious beliefs that Freud believed could be illuminated by psychoanalysis. No serious anthropologist would now give any credence to Freud's theories. Indeed, in later years, Freud himself was occasionally ambivalent about the value of the book. That it remains a surprisingly powerful work to read says more, much more, about Freud's literary abilities than his scientific ones. Sections of *Totem and Taboo* continue to have the same kind of resonance as well-told myths, a resonance that is independent of any empirical verification.

Mourning and Melancholia (1915)

Throughout his working life Freud published scientific papers and one of the most important of these was 'Mourning and Melancholia', both for the insights it provided into the conditions it studied and for the impetus it gave Freud to develop his tripartite division of the mind into id, ego and superego. Melancholia (a slightly old-fashioned term even at the time Freud used it) would now be called clinical depression and Freud was struck by the parallels between this pathological condition and the normal process of mourning. Both were characterised by what he described as 'profoundly painful dejection, cessation of interest in the outside world, loss of the capacity to love, inhibition of all activity.' In addition, in melancholia, there are often exaggerated expressions of self-loathing and an enormous sense of personal worthlessness. Freud was curious as to the origins of these feelings and pointed out that melancholia was often triggered by loss, either through death or through rejection and abandonment. And the extreme self-hatred expressed by the melancholic could be seen as a disguised form of aggression directed towards the loved one who had left them. Unable to admit the unconscious hatred that is felt for the loved one who has abandoned them, the melancholic redirect that hatred at their own egos.

Introductory Lectures on Psychoanalysis (1916-1917)

One of the most popular of Freud's works with a lay readership, these lectures, delivered at the University of Vienna Psychiatric Clinic in the winter terms of 1915-1916 and 1916-1917, aim to do exactly what the title suggests. They provide an overview and summary of Freud's ideas at the time. After an introductory lecture, in which he describes how psychoanalysis is used as a therapeutic method and asserts the central importance of the unconscious and the libido, Freud divides his lectures into three parts. Three deal with 'parapraxes', the Freudian slips of tongue and pen, the errors of forgetting and misremembering, that are dealt with most fully in *The Psychopathology of Everyday Life*. Eleven lectures are then devoted to dreams and their interpretation, outlining Freud's thoughts on the latent dream that lies behind the manifest dream, his belief that dreams are wish-fulfilments and his methods for arriving at the true interpretation, as he sees it, of the meaning of dreams. The final thirteen lectures describe his general theory of neuroses, how neurotic symptoms are rooted in unconscious mental events and in the sexual development of the individual. In 1933 Freud produced a series of New Introductory Lectures on Psychoanalysis. These recapitulate the material on dreams and dream interpretation from the earlier series but are largely concerned with the new theories of the structure of the mind and the nature of instincts with which Freud had engaged in the 1920s.

Beyond the Pleasure Principle (1920)

As the title clearly states, *Beyond the Pleasure Principle* is Freud's first attempt to move beyond his earlier belief that what motivated people was the pleasure principle (pursuit of pleasure, avoidance of pain) and that human behaviour could be explained by this pleasure principle, modified and complicated by confrontation with reality. The First World War had produced many traumatised individuals and it was clear that many of these returned again and again, in their dreams, to the events which had originally traumatised them. How could this fact be squared with any definition of the pleasure principle and its interaction with the reality principle? Freud had also noticed evidence closer to home that appeared to contradict his earlier ideas. His one-year-old grandson Heinz had devised a game which he played when his mother left him for a few hours each day. The game, involving repeatedly throwing away a toy and then retrieving it, mimicked the unpleasurable disappearance of his mother. Yet by repeatedly echoing what was unpleasurable, the child was able to gain some control over it. Perhaps this was what was happening in traumatic dreams. Repeated playing out of the original trauma was a route to exorcising the pain by gaining a new defence after the event which had not existed when it first occurred.

Yet Freud was not satisfied that he had solved the problem. What he called 'repetition-compulsion' might sometimes result in a new sense of control but it was just as likely to continue to cause suffering, even self-destruction to an individual. There was something at work 'beyond the pleasure principle' and Freud's answer was, as so often, breathtaking in its intellectual and imaginative daring. As well as Eros, the sexual instinct, there was Thanatos, the death instinct. The aim of much human activity was to reduce the tension created by instinctual demands and the impact of external reality on the individual. The demands of the sexual instinct provoked activity to reduce the tensions it created. Perhaps the death instinct, which

Freud glimpsed at work in repetition-compulsion, aimed to reduce the tensions it provoked by returning the organism to a state of inorganic inactivity i.e. death. In a bizarre way the aim of all life was, finally, death.

The Future of an Illusion (1927)

The Future of an Illusion presents Freud's ideas on religion and on the psychological origins of religion. Although he acknowledges the importance of religion as a means by which men could be persuaded to renounce fulfilment of their instinctual wishes, and although (ever the intellectual elitist) he considers that all but a few would never have agreed to the renunciation of instinct that civilisation demands without religion, Freud's lack of sympathy with religious ideas pervades the book. Religion is compared to neurosis, something to be overcome if full maturity is to be achieved. Religious practices have the same psychological roots as the rituals of obsessional neurotics. Belief in gods, and religious ideas generally, spring from man's helplessness in the face of nature. Just as the helpless child turns for protection to the father, religious believers turn to father figures that have been created for them by earlier generations in the shape of the gods. The time has now come, in Freud's opinion, for rationality to replace religious ideas. The illusions of the past should be dismissed in the same way that the healthy individual shrugs off neurosis. Freud is uncharacteristically optimistic about our ability to do this and he puts his faith in science. 'Our science is no illusion', he concludes, but it would be an illusion to continue to imagine that religion can provide something that science cannot. *The Future of an Illusion* is one of Freud's most readable books, clear in its arguments and robustly polemical at times. However, even non-believers may feel that his dismissal of religious ideas is based on a very reductive interpretation of them and that there is more that needs to be said on the subject than he allows.

Civilisation and its Discontents (1930)

In *Civilisation and Its Discontents* Freud gives fullest expression to his belief that there is a necessary and unavoidable antagonism between the demands of instinct and the restrictions that civilisation put upon them. For Freud, 'civilisation' refers to the sum total of cultural achievements and social relationships that distinguish us from all other animals. It is our protection against the often violent indifference of nature to our needs and against the aggression and violence within ourselves that threaten continually to undermine human relations. Yet this protection and security, at all times under peril, is only achieved at a cost. Our basic instincts, if followed through without restriction, would undermine civilisation. Our libido and our aggression have to be, to some extent, repressed for civilisation to work. Yet frustration is the inevitable consequence of this. The evolution of civilisation is a constant struggle between altruism and egoism, between acquiescence to society's rules and the selfish fulfilment of individual desire. One result of this is that the growth of civilisation is inextricably bound up with an increase in the sense of guilt in the individual, since he or she is aware, both consciously and unconsciously, of those destructive and transgressive desires which exist in us all. Freud concludes by pondering (with his usual, innate gloominess) the question of whether our cultural development is enough to master the underlying human instinct for aggression and self-destruction.

Moses and Monotheism (1939)

This was the last book that Freud completed before his death. It was started in the mid-1930s and was revised several times before publication, much of this work of revision coinciding with the political tensions and turmoil's in Austria which culminated in the Nazi *Anschluss*. The book was finally published in 1939 after Freud had been obliged to emigrate to Britain. *Moses and Monotheism* is as much historical speculation as anything else, although it also includes the ageing Freud's attempts at an understanding of the anti-Semitism that had driven him out of Vienna, an understanding that squared with the knowledge of the human mind he had spent a lifetime acquiring. Freud argues that Moses was, in fact, Egyptian rather than Jewish and that the Mosaic religion given to the Jews was a version of the monotheistic Aten religion, instituted by the unorthodox pharaoh Akhenaten. The Moses of the Bible was a fusion of the original Egyptian figure with a later Jewish religious innovator and Yahweh was a Midianite god given the attributes of the Egyptian Aten. The Egyptian Moses, Freud believed, had been murdered by the Jews, in a replay of the murder of the dominant male in the primal horde, as described by Freud many years earlier in *Totem and Taboo*. In much the same way as that primal parricide had led to the religious strictures of totem and taboo, so the murder of Moses had led to the adoption of the Judaic religion. And, in the same way that the primal parricide was the root cause of human guilt, so the killing of Moses gave the Jewish peoples a peculiarly strong, unconscious sense of remorse for the murder. 'It is plausible to conjecture,' Freud wrote, 'that remorse for the murder of Moses provided the stimulus for the wishful phantasy of the Messiah, who was to return and lead his people to redemption and the promised world-dominion.' Whether this is a plausible conjecture or not - indeed whether the whole of *Moses and Monotheism* is plausible or not - is arguable. Freud's gifts as a writer propels the reader through the text. However, to follow him to his conclusions demands acceptance of a number of ideas, both scientific and historical, which have been discredited since his death. This book, written when he was in his eighties and in almost constant pain, none the less shows Freud's literary skill and his lifelong willingness to 'think outside the box.'

Chapter Four: Freud's Case Histories

Anna O.

It could easily be argued that the patient known as Anna O. was the most important patient in psychoanalytic history, the first to point Freud in the direction of the 'talking-cure', a phrase she herself invented. And, ironically, she wasn't a patient of Freud at all, who never met her, but of Josef Breuer, who told Freud the details of her case in 1882. Anna O. was a highly intelligent, sexually immature woman, aged 21, who came to see Breuer at the end of 1880. She had spent much of the previous six months nursing her father through a serious illness. She had herself become seriously ill with a variety of symptoms that ranged from the partial paralysis that was familiar from other cases of hysteria through strange disruptions of speech and language to full-blown hallucinations. After the death of her father in April 1881 these symptoms became worse. During the day she was assailed by ever more vivid hallucinations before she sank, in the evening, into a kind of trance in which she muttered and mumbled what seemed to be a nonsensical melange of the several languages she knew.

Breuer was clearly a sympathetic physician, prepared to spend much time with Anna O., and he succeeded in persuading her to talk, while in her trance, about her hallucinations. Once she had described her hallucinations, she emerged from her trance feeling much better. If, for some reason, she wasn't able to describe them, the result was an increase in agitation and anxiety. Breuer had discovered that Anna's symptoms disappeared when traced back to source and could be exorcised when unpleasant events that had been forgotten were brought back to consciousness. Her hydrophobia, for example, which developed at one point in the course of treatment, was both explained and explained away when Anna, during one of her trances, recalled seeing an Englishwoman in a hotel who allowed her dog to drink out of a glass. Anna was disgusted by what she saw but politeness and social etiquette prevented her saying anything. Her disgust could only express itself, in metamorphosed form, in her hydrophobia. Once this incident was recalled, her hydrophobia disappeared.

Breuer's treatment of Anna's hysteria, with its often bewildering array of symptoms, continued for several months. Breuer moved from relying on Anna's trances to using hypnosis to probe into the causes of her symptoms. The 'talking-cure' or 'chimney-sweeping', as Anna also called it, could have proceeded to a satisfactory conclusion. Breuer, in fact, suggested to Anna that a final cure was in sight but this only revealed the extent to which the woman had become dependent on the physician. A new series of hallucinations, in which Anna claimed to be pregnant with Breuer's child, was triggered. By this time Breuer was alarmed by what was happening and he stopped treatment abruptly, decamping from Vienna for a holiday with his wife at very short notice.

Anna O., who was, in reality, a woman called Bertha Pappenheim, was left to recover as best she could. (She did recover and went on to become a renowned social worker and feminist, commemorated on an Austrian postage stamp.) The following year Breuer told his younger friend Freud about the case. During his time in Paris in the mid-1880s Freud mentioned the case to Charcot but the great neurologist seemed uninterested. It was not until 1889 that Freud returned again to the Anna O. case and persuaded a reluctant Breuer that there was more to be investigated.

'Dora'

The analysis of the young woman known as 'Dora' is important for a number of reasons. 'Dora' was sent to Freud by her father, a wealthy industrialist, in the autumn of 1900. She was eighteen and had been suffering from what were seen at the time as standard symptoms of 'hysteria.' She had fainting fits and periods of intense depression. She alternated between saying little and pouring forth her emotions in a torrent of often strange, illogical language. She threatened suicide. To Freud, by this time an expert in hysteria, these were common enough symptoms and he wrote to Fliess, in confident tones, that 'the case has smoothly opened to the existing collection of picklocks.' His patient, the teenage 'Dora', was less confident. She strenuously resisted Freud's interpretations of the events, dreams and thoughts that she confided in him and, after only a few months, terminated the analysis herself. Freud wrote up his case notes immediately and, some four years later, published *Fragment of an Analysis of a Case of Hysteria*. Despite its tentative title, and despite the fact that 'Dora's' symptoms were commonplace enough, Freud obviously placed great significance on this case history and it was soon recognised as one of the finest of his reports on individual patients. For many years it was used by students of psychoanalysis as a textbook example of how to carry out an analysis. Yet for some decades the shortcomings in Freud's treatment of 'Dora' have been apparent and feminist critics, in particular, have focussed on the case.

To see why this is so, it is necessary to look in greater detail at 'Dora's' circumstances and the interpretation that Freud placed on her symptoms, dreams etc. 'Dora' was at the centre of two emotionally troubled marriages, those of her parents and of their friends, Herr and Frau K. Frau K. was her father's mistress. 'Dora' herself had developed an adolescent crush on Frau K., whom she believed to be the only person who understood her. Herr K. had made sexual advances to 'Dora' some years previously, which she had rejected, and it was the renewal of these advances that was at the heart of her 'hysterical' breakdown. She had told her father of them but he had refused to believe her and accused her of engaging in sexual fantasy. To a dispassionate observer with the benefit of hindsight, it can seem as if Freud came very close to colluding openly with her father in denying the reality of 'Dora's' experiences. Using his new method of dream interpretation, he came to the conclusion that Dora's apparent distaste for Herr K. disguised a love for him that had been in existence for a number of years. 'Dora' was vehement in her denial of this but Freud persisted and, at her penultimate session, finally forced her to acknowledge it. It is hard not to feel repelled by the smugness with which Freud noted, 'And Dora disputed the fact no longer', after this session. It is equally hard not to feel that Freud was wrong. 'Dora' did continue to dispute the fact. Emotionally pressured, indeed bullied, by Freud and her father, she acquiesced briefly in their interpretation but it is surely significant that she brought the treatment to an abrupt conclusion as soon as she could.

Little Hans

The story of Little Hans first appeared in a paper published in 1909 called *The Analysis of a Phobia in a five-year old Boy*. The title of the paper might appear to suggest that the analysis of the five year old was carried out by Freud in much the same way as his analyses of adults - through long hours of consultation and interaction. In fact, Freud only saw Little Hans once at the time - he met him again some years later when Hans had grown up and become, like his father, a musician - and the analysis was conducted almost entirely through the medium of the boy's father, an early enthusiast for Freud's theories. The case of Little Hans presents so classic an example of the recently expounded Oedipus complex in action that it is difficult not to suspect that, occasionally, Hans' father was unconsciously tailoring the material he reported to Freud to fit what he knew of the theory. However, as the only major child analysis in Freud's works and clear evidence of infantile sexuality that was not retrospectively deduced from dreams and analysis, it is of obvious importance as a case-history.

The case began with Little Hans' fear of leaving the house. When asked why he was afraid of venturing outside, he replied that he was concerned that horses would bite him. Hans' difficulties were traced back more than a year to the time when his sister was born and he began to wonder about babies and where they came from. At the same time he began to show interest in what he called 'widdlers' - his own, other people's and, indeed, those belonging to horses, which, he could not have helped noticing in the streets of Vienna of the time, were bigger than any others. His own experiments with genital stimulation had been met with parental disapproval. ('If you do that,' his mother told him, 'I'll send for the doctor to cut off your widdler, and then what will you widdle with?' 'With my bottom,' replied the evidently resourceful Hans.) Out of all this had emerged his hippophobia.

To Freud Hans' fear of horses cried out for interpretation in the light of the Oedipus complex. Hans longed for sole possession of his mother but was afraid of how his father, possessed of a bigger penis, might react. He might castrate him or have the doctor castrate him. Hans was, however, unwilling to acknowledge the fear his father inspired and had therefore displaced this fear on to horses, possessors of the biggest penises of all. Fear of his father was transformed into fear that horses would bite him. (Hans' own explanation that he was frightened horses might bite him because somebody had told him that that was what horses did, was dismissed out of hand.) What's more, by refusing to go out, Hans gained more time to stay with his mother. Freud's solution to the problem was to advise Hans' father to be less severe on the boy's innocent interest in 'widdlers', their uses and dimensions, and even to adopt it as a reasonable topic of conversation between the two of them. If Hans sensed that his father approved of the subject and that he and his widdler would one day grow up, then the castration anxiety would disappear.

The Rat Man

The Rat Man was the name Freud gave to an unusual patient who came to see him suffering from a wide range of obsessional thoughts and rituals. The name is taken from an obsessional fear that the patient, an Army officer, expressed. While they were both on manoeuvres, a fellow officer had told him about a method of torture allegedly used in the Far East. The victim was tied down and a pot filled with rats strapped to his buttocks. With no other means of getting out, the rats eventually began to gnaw their way through the victim's anus. The Rat Man was appalled, but also fascinated by this story, and found it impossible to get it out of his mind. He had recently lost his glasses and had sent to Vienna for a new pair. Before the new pair arrived he heard the story of the rats. Immediately the idea that the rat-torture would be inflicted on his father and on the woman he loved came forcefully into his mind and could not be dislodged. The only way in which this could be avoided, he decided, was if he undertook an extraordinarily elaborate series of actions, many of them connected to the apparently simple task of paying for the new glasses he had received. If he didn't the rats would get his father, even though his father had actually been dead nine years, and also the woman he loved, although she was safe in Vienna and extremely unlikely to become the victim of a far eastern method of torture.

This was only the most *outré* example of an array of obsessional thoughts and rituals which had plagued the Rat Man since childhood. Another example also involved the woman he loved and the harm that he believed might come to her unless he undertook certain actions. She was about to leave a certain town and the Rat Man was walking the road along which her carriage would shortly travel. He saw a stone in the road and convinced himself that he had to move it, otherwise the wheel of her carriage would strike it, the carriage would overturn and she would be hurt. So he placed it elsewhere on the road. Then he decided that he had, in fact, moved the stone to a position in the road where it was *more* dangerous and *more* likely to cause an accident to his lady's carriage. So he had to pick it up again and try and replace it exactly where it had been before. These agonising decisions and changes of mind and vacillations had taken up much of the Rat Man's mental energy for years but it was the culminating horror of hearing about the rat-torture, and its effect on his thoughts, that had driven him to consult Freud.

The Rat Man's analysis lasted nearly a year and, according to Freud, he emerged from it a cured man. He had only a few years in which to enjoy his new-found mental health. He was killed early in the First World War.

Schreber

Freud's case study of Schreber (*Psychoanalytic Notes on an Autobiographical Account of a Case of Paranoia*, first published in 1911) is unusual among his case histories in that Schreber was not one of Freud's patients. Indeed they never met. Freud's analysis of Schreber's case is based almost entirely on Schreber's own book, *Memoirs of My Nervous Illness*, published in 1903. Schreber was a senior legal figure in Dresden who, intermittently, over a twenty-year period, suffered from a remarkable series of delusions. These delusions were extensive and bizarre but their central meaning to Schreber himself can be summarised simply enough. He believed that he had a mission to redeem the world, restoring it to a state of lost bliss, and he believed that he could only fulfil this mission if he was transformed from a man to a woman. Newly created as a woman, Schreber would be so desired by God that He would impregnate him and the resulting child would be the redeeming messiah.

To Freud, the hidden significance of Schreber's delusions was clear. It was related to homosexual desires that Schreber would not acknowledge. In their earliest form these unconscious homosexual feelings had been directed towards his father. Unable to reach the conscious mind, these feelings had attached to themselves to the impregnating God of Schreber's world-redeeming fantasies. To Freud, indeed, Schreber was a classic example of the paranoid personality – at various times in his illness, Schreber imagined that his doctors were undertaking horrible experiments on his body – and the paranoid personality, for Freud, was created by unresolved homosexual conflicts within it. This is not a belief that modern scientific research has supported and Freud has also been criticised for failing to investigate the circumstances of Schreber's upbringing. Had he done so, he would have discovered that Schreber's father, although an eminent doctor and educational theorist, was also a sadistic domestic tyrant who brutalised the lives of his offspring in the name of his ideas on the correct upbringing of children. Schreber's elder brother had committed suicide. Perhaps Schreber's delusions were the result of the brutality of his childhood rather than the product of unacknowledgeable homosexual fantasy.

The Wolf Man

The Wolf Man came from a wealthy, landowning Russian family and first consulted Freud in 1910, suffering from depression and a variety of obsessional symptoms. Freud treated him for four years, up until the summer before the outbreak of World War I, and again, for a few months, after the war was over in 1919 and 1920. The Wolf Man is so-called because of a childhood dream which he described vividly to Freud and which proved central to Freud's interpretation of his problems. In the dream a tree outside his bedroom window was seen to be crowded with white wolves. Freud's analysis of the dream and his reconstruction of events in the Wolf Man's childhood which lay behind it are complex, ingenious and, depending on one's viewpoint, extraordinarily insightful or exceptionally far-fetched. Freud believed that for a child to witness what he called the 'primal scene' of his parents having intercourse could have a traumatic effect on later development. This is what, by elaborate reasoning, he argued had happened to the Wolf Man. Furthermore, and again using inventive elaboration from the 'wolf-dream', Freud said that, as a child of less than two years old, the Wolf Man, lying in his cot, had seen his father taking his mother from behind.

The Wolf Man lived on into old age and an interesting postscript to his case is provided by his own thoughts on Freud and analysis as recorded in a number of interviews undertaken in the last few years before his death in 1979 at the age of 92. They provide a fascinating opportunity to assess how an analysis with Freud appeared to the person under analysis. The Wolf Man, looking back, had little time for Freud's interpretation of his dream. 'When he interprets the white wolves as nightshirts or something like that, for example linen sheets or clothes,' he told one interviewer, 'that's somehow far-fetched, I think. That scene in the dream where the windows open and so on and the wolves are sitting there, and his interpretation, I don't know, these things are miles apart. It's terribly far-fetched.' Yet the Wolf Man had no doubts about Freud's stature as both man and thinker. It is clear that he believed that his time under analysis by Freud had been one of the most significant periods of his life and that Freud was 'a genius, there's no denying it. All those ideas that he combined in a system.'

Chapter Five: Freud's Family, Friends, Colleagues And Fellow Early Analysts

Karl Abraham (1877 - 1925)

Born into a bourgeois family in Bremen, North Germany, Karl Abraham studied medicine and then specialised in psychiatry. He first encountered Freud's ideas through Jung with whom he worked at the Burgholzli Clinic near Zurich and first met Freud personally in 1907. Abraham was an immediate convert to psychoanalytic theory and was to prove a valuable colleague to Freud. Returning to Germany, Abraham founded the Berlin Institute of Psychoanalysis in 1910. At first the Institute had only five members but it survived and even prospered, becoming the model for similar institutes throughout the world. Abraham was one of the most important figures in the growth of psychoanalysis in Germany and his early death, while still in his forties, was a blow both to Freud personally and to the psychoanalytic movement.

Alfred Adler (1870 – 1937)

Adler was one of the first appreciative readers of Freud's *magnum opus*, *The Interpretation of Dreams*, one of the founder members of the Wednesday Discussion Society and one of the first to find Freud's insistence on intellectual submission too constraining. Born and educated in Vienna, he was a well-respected doctor, working in one of the poorer areas of the city when he came across Freud's book and made contact with the older man. Adler, with his striking intelligence and willingness to think unconventionally, was a valued member of the early psychoanalytic movement but, ironically, it was these very qualities that were to lead to the break with Freud. Although inspired by much of Freud's thinking, Adler was always uneasy with the idea that neurosis could be explained exclusively by sexual trauma. Although he published work which clearly demonstrated his differences with Freud, the friendship was maintained for a number of years. By 1911, however, the rift was too wide to bridge. At Freud's instigation, Adler was expelled from the Vienna Psychoanalytic Society of which he had only recently been president. He formed his own group, initially called the Society for Free Psychoanalytic Inquiry. In later years Adler was to develop further his own theories of what he called 'Individual Psychology' and divided his time between his native Vienna and the United States, where his ideas have been greatly influential. He and Freud never met after the 1911 falling out but, from a historical perspective, it is clear that Adler was, apart from Jung, the most gifted and original of the early psychoanalysts.

Minna Bernays (1865 – 1941)

Minna Bernays was Freud's sister-in-law, the younger sibling of his wife Martha, and the subject of much speculation (of varying degrees of prurience) by biographers. Was Minna Freud's lover at any time? Did she, indeed, become pregnant by Freud and have an abortion? Certainly she and Freud were close. From 1895 she lived with the family at 19 Berggasse. Freud enjoyed her company and they took several holidays together over the years. In most ways, the more intellectual Minna was better suited to the role of Freud's confidante about his work than the conventional, rather prudish Martha. Perhaps the two were lovers. With both of them long dead, and no documentary evidence in existence, it is impossible to say one way or the other. However, it is as well to remember that most of the circumstantial evidence comes either from convoluted readings of Freud's own writings or from alleged remarks made by Jung decades after the supposed events. Jung is reported to have said, in 1957, that, when he visited Berggasse fifty years earlier, Minna confided in him that she and Freud had had a sexual relationship. 'From her,' he told a colleague, 'I learned that Freud was in love with her and that their relationship was indeed very intimate.' Jung was an extraordinarily charismatic man, able to coax the truth from even the most reticent of people, and it is possible that Minna chose to tell her secret to him. However, his remarks are pretty unconvincing even as hearsay and the case remains very much unproven. All we know is that Minna remained unmarried and lived in Berggasse until events drove the Freud family into exile. She died in London in 1941.

Marie Bonaparte (1882 – 1962)

The great grand-niece of the Emperor Napoleon I and the wife of Prince George of Greece might seem an unlikely convert to psychoanalysis. However, this highly intelligent, very wealthy but deeply troubled woman became one of Freud's closest confidantes in his last years, published extensively on psychoanalytic subjects and was one of the principal early promoters of Freudian ideas in France. Marie Bonaparte was born in July 1882. Her father was the grandson of Napoleon's brother Lucien. Her mother, who died a few weeks after Marie's birth, came from an immensely wealthy family of entrepreneurs. Marie grew up the archetypal 'poor little rich girl', wanting for nothing but the love that she continued to seek all her life. Married to the son of the king of Greece, she took several lovers (including the charismatic French politician Aristide Briand) but was still, in her early forties, searching for some core belief to give meaning to her life when she first read Freud. Immediately sensing that here was something to which she could commit her forceful personality and intelligence, she asked a mutual friend to arrange psychoanalytic treatment for her with Freud. Freud was initially reluctant (perhaps suspecting she was some spoilt and silly aristocrat in search of the latest fad) but he agreed to see her in September 1925. It was the start of what became a fruitful relationship for both of them. Freud gained a prominent and energetic champion for his ideas in France, and both he and his movement received generous financial help from the Princess' fortune. When the Nazis arrived in Vienna, it was largely due to Marie Bonaparte's connections, wealth and determination that Freud and his family were able to escape to England. Marie Bonaparte herself gained a focus for her energies and her intellectual gifts. She became a central figure in the psychoanalytic movement and published many books and papers on subjects as various as female sexuality and criminal psychology. Not the least of her services to the movement was her purchase of the Freud-Fliess letters and her adamant refusal to surrender them to Freud, who would undoubtedly have destroyed them. Without her willingness to buy the letters and then to withstand the request of the man she admired more than any other, the early history of Freud's psychoanalytic thinking would be lost to us.

Josef Breuer (1842 - 1925)

Breuer has sometimes been called the 'grandfather of psycho-analysis'. Fourteen years older than Freud, he had had a distinguished career since the 1860s (when he had described a reflex involved in the control of normal breathing which is still called the Hering-Breuer reflex) and was a much-respected figure in Viennese medical circles. It was Breuer who had, in 1880, relieved the hysterical symptoms of the patient known as Anna O. by getting her to recollect traumatic experiences under hypnosis. It was Breuer who, two years later, had told Freud about this case and about his ideas that neurotic symptoms were the result of unconscious processes and could be cured by bringing the unconscious into consciousness. And initially, in their collaboration on the book *Studies in Hysteria*, it was Breuer who was the senior partner. It was only as the investigations into hysteria began to lead onto what appeared dangerous ground that Breuer - older, more cautious, with a greater reputation to risk - began to take second place to Freud. Freud was convinced that hysteria and hysterical symptoms were sexual in origin. Breuer was increasingly resistant to the notion that they were exclusively sexual in nature and concerned about the direction in which Freud's ideas were leading. It was on this fundamental disagreement that Freud and Breuer's collaboration foundered about the time of the first publication of *Studies in Hysteria*. They rarely saw one another after 1896, although, when Breuer died in 1925, Freud wrote a largely generous obituary notice of his former colleague.

Sandor Ferenczi (1873 – 1933)

The Hungarian Sandor Ferenczi was one of the most loyal and the most trusted of all Freud's early colleagues. He wrote to Freud from Budapest in 1907, expressing admiration for psychoanalytic ideas, was a delegate at the first congress of psychoanalysts in Salzburg the following year and was soon a family friend as well as a colleague. In 1909 Ferenczi joined Freud and Jung on the momentous visit to lecture in America. (Perversely, Freud, who was intolerant of dissension from his views, was also irritated by Ferenczi's deference to him. He wrote to Jung, about a later trip he made with Ferenczi to Italy, 'My travelling companion is a dear fellow...but his attitude to me is infantile. He never stops admiring me, which I don't like.') For the next twenty years Ferenczi was one of Freud's most regular correspondents and carved out a career for himself as a successful and respected psychoanalyst. He trained several analysts who were later to become famous in their own right, including Melanie Klein. Towards the end of his life, even this most orthodox of Freud's followers began to express ideas at odds with those of the movement's founding father. His death, in 1933, was a severe blow to Freud but may well have prevented another of those splits which litter the history of psychoanalysis. A paper Ferenczi had delivered to the annual conference of the International Psychoanalytic Association the previous year had been met coldly by Freud because it appeared to reassert the possibility that 'child seduction' stories provided by patients described reality rather than fantasy. This notion Freud had dismissed in the 1890s and he had no wish to see it resurface. Ferenczi's death meant that controversy could be avoided.

Wilhelm Fliess (1858-1928)

During the 1890s, when Freud was elaborating the fundamental ideas of psychoanalysis, one of the very few people who combined professional and personal support at a time of great isolation was the Berlin doctor Wilhelm Fliess. Fliess and Freud did not meet very often, but between 1893 and 1904, they corresponded frequently. Fliess was an ear nose and throat specialist who had developed idiosyncratic notions of his own about the origins of disease. He believed that many illnesses, especially sexual ones, could be traced back to disturbances in the mucous membranes of the nose. In the context of the medical knowledge of the time, this was not as bizarre as it may now seem. Fliess was drawing on research and ideas that were, at the time, unconventional but not beyond the pale. However it is clear that, at the time, both Fliess and Freud were both working at the very fringes of conventional medicine where the boundary between daring, innovative thinking and crackpot charlatanry was not always clearly delineated. Each gave the other badly-needed moral support. Their friendship even survived a disastrous episode in 1895 in which a patient, referred to Fliess by Freud, nearly died as a result of the Berlin physician's incompetence and insistence on explaining everything by means of his offbeat theories. Freud must, at some level, have acknowledged to himself how misguided Fliess was in the treatment of this patient but such was his need for a sympathetic colleague and a sounding-board for his own ideas that he ignored any misgivings he might have had. As Freud gained confidence in his own theories, he and Fliess drifted apart. Their correspondence ended in 1904 in mutual accusations of betrayal and Freud took to suggesting that his former confidant was a man suffering from paranoia. Fliess died in 1928.

Anna Freud (1895-1982)

Anna, the youngest of Freud's six children, was the only one to follow him into psychoanalysis as a profession. As a teenager she read some her father's work but it was only after the First World War that she began to train seriously as an analyst. Her father undertook her analysis in 1920 (something strictly against later psychoanalytic best practice which bars close relations entering the analyst/analysand relationship) and she became a member of the Vienna Psychoanalytical Society in 1922. The following year she started her own psychoanalytic practice and was soon specialising in the analysis of children, the area in which she was to undertake her most original work over the next half century. Unmarried and devoted to her father, Anna became Freud's nurse during the succession of painful illnesses and operations that plagued the last decade and a half of his life. After his death she not only continued her own work in child psychology but also became the guardian of her father's memory and of Freudian orthodoxy. She died in 1982 and the house in Maresfield Gardens, Hampstead, where her father had spent the last year of his life and where she lived for more than forty years, became the Freud Museum.

Martha Freud (née Bernays) (1861 – 1951)

Martha Bernays, Freud's future wife, came from a distinguished Jewish family, one made up of far more conspicuous achievers than her future husband's. Her grandfather was Chief Rabbi in Hamburg and two of her uncles were well-known German academics. Her father, a merchant, moved to Vienna when Martha was a child (after a financial scandal, according to some sources.) Freud first met Martha when she visited his sisters in April 1882 and, within a short time, their feelings for one another were strong. They were engaged (unofficially) in the middle of June. For various reasons, largely financial, they were unable to marry for more than four years and, during this period, Freud wrote many hundreds of love letters to his fiancée which are testimony both to the strength of his feelings for her and a possessive jealousy that, masked though it often is by his habitual irony, sometimes verges on the pathological. Finally married in both civil and religious ceremonies in September, the Freuds entered a life of apparent bourgeois domesticity that was to last until his death in 1939. They produced six children, the last of whom, Anna, was born in 1895. Martha looked after the home and the children. Several witnesses attest to her remarkable lack of knowledge of her husband's ground-breaking work and to an equal lack of interest in it. The image both wished to present to the world was one of conventional marital happiness. To Freud, Martha was 'an adored sweetheart in youth, and a beloved wife in maturity.' Martha, in a letter to a granddaughter, wrote, 'I wish for you to be as fortunate in your marriage as I have been in mine. For during the fifty three years I was married to your grandfather, there was never an unfriendly look or a harsh word between us.' Perhaps the marriage was as stress-free as both claimed. In the absence of the kind of documentary evidence that records their courtship and long engagement, it is impossible to know. Rumours about Freud's relationship with his sister-in-law Minna Bernays and speculation about intellectual incompatibility between himself and Martha can be nothing more than rumour and speculation. What is undoubtedly true is that

Freud cherished the domestic space that his marriage and his wife provided him. It was a safe bastion amid the troubled waters of his controversial career. Despite the adventurousness of his thinking, he looked to have a private life of quiet respectability and this Martha provided.

Otto Gross (1877 – 1920)

Otto Gross is one of the most interesting of the early adherents of psychoanalysis, a man Freud's biographer Ernest Jones was to describe as 'the nearest approach to the romantic ideal of a genius I have ever met.' He saw psychoanalysis, which he discovered in 1904, as one more tool in the struggle to free man from the tyranny of a patriarchal, capitalist society. Yet he is largely forgotten today and he has been neatly excised from many of the histories of the early movement. It is not difficult to see why. Gross, the son of a world-renowned Austrian criminologist, was a drug-addicted, sexually promiscuous anarchist. To Freud, who was, despite the adventurousness of his thinking, solidly bourgeois and respectable, Gross, like Wilhelm Reich later, represented the unacceptable face of psychoanalysis. Yet Gross, with his co-option of psychoanalysis into a wider struggle against political and social oppression, was an interesting thinker. Even Freud was moved to write to Jung (who was engaged in a confusing analysis of Gross in which Gross repeatedly insisted on turning the tables and attempting to analyse Jung) that Gross had 'such a fine mind.' Regularly incarcerated because of his addiction, his supposed mental instability and his dangerous political ideas, Gross eventually died, broken and destitute, on the streets of Berlin. He deserves re-examination and his influence on the social and artistic avant-garde of his time (he knew everybody from the psychoanalysts to the Dadaists to Franz Kafka) should be re-assessed.

Ernest Jones (1879 - 1958)

Not only did Ernest Jones, in effect, introduce psychoanalysis to Britain but he was also Freud's official biographer. On Jones' fiftieth birthday, Freud wrote to him, 'I have always numbered you among my inmost family', and Jones remained committed to the Freudian cause throughout his life. Born near Glamorgan, Jones studied in Cardiff and London and research work in neurology brought him into contact with Freud's writings, then little known outside Austria and Germany. Jones was an immediate convert and he was soon a personal friend of the founder of psychoanalysis. In 1913 he founded the British Psychoanalytical Society and in 1920 the International Journal of Psychoanalysis, which he edited for thirteen years. His biography of Freud was published in the 1950s

Carl Gustav Jung (1875 – 1961)

Such has been Jung's growing fame and influence in the nine decades since his split with Freud that the importance to him of the older man has often been overlooked. Jungians have a tendency either to ignore or to underestimate the relationship, both personal and intellectual, between the two men. Yet, for just over six years, Jung and Freud were exceptionally close. The son of a Swiss Lutheran pastor, Jung studied medicine at the University of Basel and first encountered Freud's ideas in 1906 when he was working at the Burghölzli Institute outside Zurich, one of the most prestigious psychiatric institutes in Europe. Immediately impressed by what he read, Jung wrote to Freud to express his admiration. Freud, delighted that his work was reaching an appreciative professional audience outside the tightly-knit circle of the first psychoanalysts in Vienna, wrote back and, very shortly, the relationship became enormously significant for both men. From the beginning the tensions that were eventually to drive the two apart were apparent to both of them. In a letter of 1907, while expressing 'boundless admiration' for Freud, Jung acknowledged that 'my veneration for you has something of the character of a religious "crush". Yet he was also writing, in the preface to one of his books, that 'Fairness to Freud does not imply, as many fear, unqualified submission to a dogma; one can very well maintain an independent judgement.' As events were to prove, Freud often did require 'unqualified submission' and was not always appreciative of 'an independent judgement'. Initially, however, the relationship, conducted through letters and through personal meetings, was productive for both men. Jung became the 'crown prince' of the psychoanalytic movement, accompanying Freud on the 1909 trip to America and being elected president of the International Psychoanalytic Association the following year. The first major strain in the relationship occurred in 1912 when Jung returned to the States to deliver a series of lectures in which, while ostensibly defending Freudian ideas, he made clear his own reservations about the centrality of sexuality to them. To

Freud this was heresy but a charged meeting at a Munich hotel (at one point Freud fell to the floor in a faint and had to be carried to his room by Jung) seemed to result in reconciliation. This was only paper-thin, however. The very qualities that Freud admired in Jung – his originality and intellectual drive – continued to force the younger man to question what was fast becoming psychoanalytic orthodoxy and, indeed, dogma. By 1913 Jung could no longer contain his criticisms of Freud. In a letter that effectively ended their personal relationship, he wrote that Freud's 'technique of treating your pupils like patients is a blunder….You go about sniffing out all the symptomatic actions in your vicinity, thus reducing everyone to the level of sons and daughters who blushingly admit the existence of their faults. Meanwhile you remain on top as the father, sitting pretty.' The following year he resigned from the presidency of the International Psychoanalytic Association and from his position as editor of the movement's major journal. He had embarked on the difficult personal and intellectual journey which was, ultimately, to lead to his own greatest achievements.

Otto Rank (1884 - 1939)

For nearly twenty years Otto Rank was one of the closest of Freud's associates. Born in Vienna as Otto Rosenfeld, he chose the name Rank in his teens as a means both of self-invention and repudiation of a father he despised. Rank came to Freud's attention after reading *The Interpretation of Dreams* and submitting an essay to its author which made use of psychoanalytic ideas. Freud was sufficiently impressed that, in 1906, Rank was appointed secretary to the Vienna Psychoanalytic Society. For the next twenty years Rank was at the heart of the rapidly-developing movement, as a prolific and gifted writer, an editor and one of the founders of the International Psychoanalytic Association. Through the often traumatic crises in the movement, such as the bitter departures of Adler and Jung, Rank remained loyal to Freud. However, in the early 1920s, Rank drifted further and further into what Freud saw as heresy and publication of Rank's *The Trauma of Birth* in 1924 signalled the final rupture in a relationship that had meant much to both men.

Wilhelm Reich (1897-1957)

Reich is now best known in his later incarnation as the promoter of the ill-defined 'orgone energy' which he claimed could cure almost all known ailments. Half guru, half-quack Reich was persecuted by the American authorities in the 1950s (he died in an American prison) yet given posthumous recognition in the 1960s as one of the prophets of the Permissive Society. As a younger man, he was one of the great hopes of the psychoanalytic movement and yet another of the many acolytes who, ultimately, disappointed Freud. Born in Galicia in 1897, to a middle-class Jewish family, Reich was unusual among the early analysts (indeed among any analysts) in that he had suffered terrible, and very real, emotional pain in a family tragedy of sex and death. As a child he had witnessed the affair between his mother and his tutor. His father had discovered the affair and his mother had committed suicide. After the First World War Reich trained in medicine and became involved in psychoanalysis even before graduating. He set up a psychoanalytic practice and Freud, who thought highly of him, was soon referring patients to him. Reich's unorthodoxy, however, was always apparent and the relationship between the two men rapidly became strained. As with Otto Gross, before the war, Freud was keen to distance himself and the movement he had founded from a maverick whose ideas and practices provided such obvious targets for critics. Reich was expelled from the movement in the early 1930s. His life and safety in Germany, where he was living and working, were soon under threat from the Nazis and he embarked on the peripatetic career which was finally to land him in fatal trouble with American Puritanism in 1957.

Wilhelm Stekel (1868 – 1940)

Stekel, a doctor and journalist, first met Freud as a patient in 1901. The following year he reviewed *The Interpretation of Dreams* for a Viennese newspaper, claiming that it marked a 'new era in psychology'. Stekel wanted to be a part of that new era. He began work as an analyst himself and was one of the founder members of the 'Wednesday Society' that first met in Freud's rooms in Berggasse in 1902. Stekel remained an important figure in the fledgling movement for the next decade but he was also a close associate of Alfred Adler, helping him to launch a journal, the *Zentralblatt für Psychoanalyse*, which became a focus for those early psychoanalysts who began to find Freud too intellectually dictatorial. When Adler broke with Freud in 1911, Stekel sided with the former and was expelled from the Vienna Psychoanalytical Society of which he was, by then, vice-president. Stekel returned to the fold in later years but he was never again close to Freud. He fled Vienna when the Nazis arrived in 1938 and, two years later, committed suicide in a London hotel room.

Chapter Six: Freud's Legacy

Why does Freud continue to matter? His ideas are, necessarily, rooted in the particular historical and cultural circumstances in which he developed them and, although he prided himself on his rigour as a scientist, many of them have been shown to have little or no basis in genuine science. Some of them seem far-fetched, wrong-headed, outmoded. Yet, whatever criticisms are directed against Freud and his ideas about the structure of the mind, it is still abundantly clear that he revolutionised the way we think about ourselves. In one of his more immodest, but not necessarily untrue statements, Freud claimed that he had dealt the last of three blows to man's pride. The first was Copernicus' revelation that the earth is not at the centre of the cosmos. The second was Darwin's proof that we were not the result of a special, divine creation but the products of a natural process – evolution – which required no intervention on God's part. Freud provided a further reason for humility by showing how little we were in control of our own thought processes. The unconscious mind was just as important as consciousness, if not more so. Probably few people today would argue that he was 'right' in the details of how the unconscious worked but, surely, even fewer would deny altogether the significance of unconscious processes. Freud's achievement was such that it is difficult to assess the extent of his influence today. Ideas about the human mind, human motivations and human development that can be traced back to him are simply all-pervasive in Western culture. As W.H. Auden wrote in a poem on Freud's death, 'to us he is no more a person/now but a whole climate of opinion.' Even the most vociferous of Freud's critics often find themselves irresistibly drawn into using terminology and patterns of thought that he created.

It is easy to criticise Freud's thinking. Quite clearly he was not the rigorous scientist he imagined himself to be. As one of his patients, the Wolf Man, said in later life of Freud's interpretations of his dreams, 'It's all so far-fetched.' Yet it's as well to remember what the Wolf Man went on to say to the woman who interviewed him. Freud was 'a genius, there's no denying it.' Put aside Freud's elaborately convoluted and ingenious interpretations of dreams and thought processes, often designed to show how they agreed with previously stated Freudian doctrine. Put aside the arguable theories of sexual development, particularly his patriarchal views of female sexuality. Ignore the anthropological just-so stories he told in books like *Totem and Taboo* to explain the origins of human behaviour, stories which later research in the human sciences have long since discredited. Forget the failed attempts to provide a physical and neurological model of the mind which would dovetail with his ideas about our psychology.

Look instead at the larger concepts that Freud was the first to pursue and look at their implications. And think about what the twentieth century (and early twenty first century) view of human nature would be without Freud. We would be largely unfamiliar with the notion of the unconscious mind. We would not be prepared to admit that large parts of our behaviour had their origins in unconscious processes. We would still be denying that sexuality and sexual impulses dated back to childhood and that adult sexuality was often deeply affected by these. We would not have fully taken on board the idea that mental problems and the distress they cause could be alleviated simply by talking about them and the associations they brought to mind. We would have very different views of dreams and what they might symbolise, of what errors and mistakes might tell us and of what was going on beneath the surface of everyday human relations. Freudian ideas have so saturated western culture, he has become so much 'the whole climate of opinion' of Auden's poem that it is almost impossible to think ourselves back to a pre-Freudian mindset. Many of the details of Freud's ideas can be criticised, put on one side, even mocked. His legacy, however, is that, as a result of his work, we have a different sense of what it is to be human, to have a mind and emotions and to interact with others.

Chapter Seven: A Short Glossary Of Freudian Ideas And Concepts

Abreaction - this is the process by which a painful emotion, repressed often for many years, can be released and its unconscious power over the individual exorcised, by replaying in the mind the original experience that gave rise to it. It played an important role in Freud's ideas from the very early days of his collaboration with Breuer. In *Studies in Hysteria* they wrote that, 'we found, to our great surprise at first, that each individual hysterical symptom immediately and permanently disappeared when we had succeeded in bringing clearly to light the memory of the event by which it was provoked and in arousing its accompanying affect, and when the patient had described that event in the greatest possible detail and had put the affect into words.' It is one of the cornerstones of psychoanalysis. No abreaction, no psychoanalysis. Or at least none with any claim to a curative power.

Affect - generally Freud used 'affect' to mean the emotional charge or feeling that attached itself to an idea or a group of ideas or an object in the external world

Castration complex - during the Oedipal phase a boy's rivalry with his father for the love of his mother induces the anxiety that the father, using his greater power and status, will have him castrated. For those fixated at the Oedipal phase this 'castration complex' can continue into adulthood

Cathexis - taken from the Greek word for 'holding', this word was much used by Freud to denote the accumulation of mental energy that could attach itself to a particular idea or memory or object

Condensation - one of the mechanisms by means of which the latent dream can hide behind the manifest dream. In condensation one idea or image in the manifest dream can represent a whole series of ideas in the latent dream. As Freud wrote in *The Interpretation of Dreams*, 'Dreams are brief, meagre and laconic in comparison with the range and wealth of the dream-thoughts.' Only through association can the ideas behind the condensed image or idea be revealed.

Death instinct or Thanatos - Freud's early theories about instinctual conflict between the pleasure principle and the reality principle never entirely satisfied him. Even after he had decided that conflict between the two was only superficial since both were aiming at the same goal - the reduction of tension - he remained unsatisfied. How could this theory possibly explain self-threatening behaviour such as masochism? The First World War brought another phenomenon demanding of explanation. Victims of shell shock were regularly reported to suffer recurring nightmares in which they re-lived, with similar feelings of terror, the same traumatic incidents that had triggered the shell shock. This was in direct contradiction to Freud's ideas about one of the purposes of dreams. As well as being the vehicles of wish-fulfilment, dreams were there to rework emotionally distressing material so that it did not disturb sleep. Yet these traumatised soldiers were repeating a deeply distressing experience time and again. How could this repetition-compulsion fit in with the pleasure principle? After thinking long and hard about repetition-compulsion, Freud was forced to the conclusion that it was a manifestation of an instinct in direct contradiction to the life instinct or the pleasure principle. This was Thanatos (from the Greek word for 'death'), the death instinct or those impulses aimed at destruction or an escape from all stimulation into a state of inorganic inertia

Displacement - the mechanism, particularly in dreams, by which a strong and troubling emotion is detached from its real cause and placed on another, often trivial, one

Dream work - the processes by which the dreamer alters the content of his or her dream in order to render it less disturbing and anxiety-provoking. These processes include condensation, displacement and symbolisation.

Ego - (taken from the Latin word for 'I') that part of Freud's tripartite division of the mind which represents the conscious self, the part which reacts to the stimuli of the external world. The ego is in constant conflict with the tumultuous, instinctual demands of the id.

Freud used a number of analogies to describe the relationship between ego and id. Perhaps most tellingly he compared the id to a horse and the ego to its rider

Electra complex - the female equivalent of the Oedipus complex in which the daughter harbours incestuous feelings towards the father and murderous antagonism to the mother. In Greek mythology Electra was the daughter of Agamemnon and Clytemnestra. After Agamemnon's return from the Trojan Wars, his wife murdered him. Electra incited her brother Orestes to kill Clytemnestra in order to revenge their father's death.

Fixation - in Freud's scheme of libidinal development there were several stages through which the individual needed to pass, several hurdles on the road to sexual maturity. A fixation occurs if the individual fails to clear one of these developmental hurdles and becomes fixated at one of the stages, attached to objects appropriate to that stage

Free association - one of the foundations of psychoanalytical practice. By encouraging the analysand to speak aloud his or stream of consciousness, one idea linking with another, one word or image suggesting another, the analyst aims to uncover unconscious thought processes that would otherwise remain hidden.

Freudian slip, *more correctly known as parapraxis* - this is one of the most familiar of Freudian ideas to the man or woman in the street and he introduced it in his 1905 book, *The Psychopathology of Everyday Life*. Freud proposed that the mind makes no meaningless errors. Slips of the tongue or of the pen on the page and failures of memory in everyday life are not mere matters of chance. They reveal hidden motivations and unconscious processes at work which can be revealed by careful analysis. One of the most telling examples of secret reasons behind temporary amnesia came from Freud's own experience. For many days in a row, despite reminding himself that he needed to buy some 'Loschpapier' (blotting paper), Freud forgot to do so. Why? he asked himself and came up with the answer that, when in the shop, he used the word 'Fliesspapier' (another German word for blotting paper) rather than 'Loschpapier'. It was the time of the painful break up of his friendship with Wilhelm Fliess and asking for 'Fliesspapier' in the shop would inevitably carry unpleasant associations. So, to avoid these, Freud simply forgot to go.

Id *in German 'das Es'* - that part of the mind, in Freud's schematic division of it into three, which is primitive, instinctual and constitutes the unconscious. Amoral and demanding of instant gratification of the libido, the id is in constant conflict with the realism of the ego and the conscience of the superego

Introjection - the process by which one absorbs an external object, or more frequently another person, into one's mind and creates a mental state which reflects that external object or person

Latent dream - the hidden and repressed ideas, wishes and desires that lurk beneath the manifest dream, waiting to be revealed by the interpretative techniques of psychoanalysis

Libido - in psychoanalytic theory, the sexual drive and energy which is directed towards individuals and objects in the outside world. Neurotic and other psychiatric illnesses are often the result of libido that is inappropriately directed.

Manifest dream - what the dreamer remembers of a dream and describes to the analyst, the raw and sometimes bizarre material from which the latent dream, with its often dark, instinctual desires, can be coaxed

Oedipus complex - the story of Oedipus is one of the most familiar and resonant of the Greek myths. King Laius of Thebes and his wife Jocasta are about to become parents when it is foretold that the child will grow up to murder his father and marry his mother. Anxious to avoid this undesirable future, Laius arranges for his new-born son to be left on a mountainside to die. Shepherds take pity on the child and rescue him. Eventually, by one of those roundabout set of circumstances so essential to any good myth, the boy is brought up by the king and queen of Corinth and named Oedipus. Ignorant of who he really is, Oedipus, as a young man, leaves Corinth when the Delphic Oracle repeats the prediction about killing his father and marrying his mother. On the road to Thebes he meets Laius by chance, they quarrel and Oedipus ends by killing the man he does not realise is his own father. Travelling onwards he defeats the Sphinx, which has been troubling the city, by correctly deciphering her riddle. Made the new king of Thebes, he marries the widow of the old king, his own mother Jocasta. When the truth finally emerges Oedipus blinds himself and Jocasta hangs herself. The reason that this myth has such resonance, according to Freud, is that it dramatises the three-way love triangle that exists in everyone's early childhood. The child falls in love with the mother, longs for total possession of her, becomes frantically jealous of the father and fantasises about killing him so that the mother is the child's alone. This fantasy of early childhood, reflected so accurately in the myth, is what Freud named the Oedipus Complex.

Parapraxis *see* Freudian slip

Penis envy - just as small boys, in the midst of Oedipal conflict, suffer from castration anxiety, so little girls develop penis envy, according to Freud. Both boys and girls take their mother as their first love-object. Whereas for boys the result is phallic comparison with the father and fear that the father will cut off the competition, for girls the result is the discovery that they are already minus the all-important phallus. Thus they come to envy what they do not possess. Unsurprisingly this idea, with its assumption of a male norm from which the female is a deviation, has not worn well and has been attacked not only by feminist writers but by a whole array of psycho-analysts

Pleasure principle - the primitive instinct in the new-born child that is directed exclusively to the gratification (in reality or fantasy) of the immediate desire for pleasure and the avoidance of pain. The pleasure principle rapidly comes into conflict with the developing 'reality principle' (see below)

Reality principle - as a child develops, it comes to be aware that the world is not, as it originally thought, centred on itself and its needs. There is a real world out there which also makes demands and there is a need to adapt one's view of the world to accommodate them. In

Freudian terms, the child needs to acknowledge the 'reality principle'.

Regression - a return to earlier stages of sexual and individual development in an attempt to avoid anxiety and psychic pain

Repression - the process by which unacceptable impulses, ideas, memories and emotions, products of the conflict between the pleasure principle and the reality principle, are forced into the unconscious. There they remain active, influencing action and experience, without themselves returning to consciousness

Resistance - the opposition that the analysand mounts to the analyst's interpretations during analysis in order to defend what has been repressed and prevent the analysis bringing unconscious material to consciousness

Screen memory - this is Freud's term for childhood memories which have escaped the filters of repression and remain as idle and fleeting impressions in the adult mind. All too often these are acting as a 'screen', masking more painful memories which it is the job of analyst and analysand to bring to consciousness.

Secondary elaboration - when one wakes, one's memories of dreams are partial, confused and lack narrative coherence. The temptation is to fill the gaps, sort out the confusions and provide a coherent narrative. This is secondary elaboration.

Sublimation - the unconscious mental process by which instinctual, socially unacceptable energy or libido is transferred to a non-instinctual, socially acceptable activity e.g. Freud believed that the sublimation of unsatisfied libido was behind the creation of great art and literature

Super-ego - that part of the mind, in Freud's division of it into id, ego and super-ego, which incorporates parental standards and social rules, thus creating conscience and obedience to externally applied laws and regulations. 'The long period of childhood, during which the growing human being lives in dependence on his parents, leaves behind it as a precipitate the formation in his ego of a special agency in which this parental influence is prolonged. It has received the name of super-ego.' (Freud)

Symbolisation - the process by which symbols are created in dreams so that repressed material can emerge in symbolic form. Most frequently the symbolism is sexual and representative of the male or female genitals. In *Introductory Lectures on Psychoanalysis* and elsewhere, Freud reveals the extraordinary range of symbols that he believes can be employed. For the male genitals these include: sticks, umbrellas, posts, trees, knives, daggers, pistols, watering-cans, pencils, hammers, snakes, hats, cigars and so on. 'The female genitals,' writes Freud, 'are symbolically represented by all such objects as share their characteristic of enclosing a hollow space which can take something into itself' and goes on to list: pits, cavities, bottles, boxes, trunks, cases, pockets, rooms, snails, mussels, churches and gates amongst others.

Transference - the process during analysis in which the analysand develops strong feelings of love, hate etc. for the analyst. These feelings derive from the traumas and dramas of the analysand's past and the analyst takes the part played previously by father, mother, siblings etc. Transference is essential to the therapeutic process and provides the analysand with the opportunity to work through repressed and unconscious material

Unconscious - those parts of the mind of which the individual is unaware. There are thoughts and ideas which are unconscious but which can be brought to consciousness fairly readily. There are others which have been systematically repressed by the individual and can only be brought to the surface after severe resistance has been overcome. This is the unconscious in which Freud was largely interested and which he believed psychoanalysis was uniquely suited to reveal. The idea of the unconscious mind was not invented by Freud. Earlier writers, as far back as the 5th century BC, had been aware that human behaviour could not be explained solely as the result of conscious mental processes. In the 19th century many writers, from philosophers to scientists, had speculated about the nature of the unconscious. The German physician C.G. Carus, a friend of Goethe, wrote, in a book first published in 1846, 'The key to the knowledge of the nature of the soul's conscious life lies in the realm of the unconscious.' Although Freud, strict materialist that he was, might not have used the word 'soul', he might otherwise have reiterated Carus' idea verbatim half-a-century later. Freud is significant because he took the unconscious so seriously, was prepared to build a theory of human nature on the basis of his ideas about it and was so successful in promulgating that theory that for fifty years and more it has been impossible to think about the unconscious without, to a greater or less extent, incorporating Freud's ideas.

Further Resources

Freud's Writings

As for most great figures in the history of thought, there exists, for Freud, a comprehensive academic edition. In German this is *Gesammelte Werke*, now published by Fischer Verlag in 18 volumes. In English it is *The Standard Edition of the Complete Psychological Works of Sigmund Freud*, produced in 24 volumes between 1953 and 1974, under the general editorship of James Strachey (younger brother of Bloomsbury biographer Lytton Strachey) and with full co-operation and collaboration from Freud's daughter Anna.

The Penguin Freud (15 volumes) - These paperback volumes constitute a very generous selection of Freud's complete works and include all the major works from *Studies in Hysteria* through *The Interpretation of Dreams* to the later writings on culture and society.

The Essentials of Psychoanalysis, Penguin, A selection from Freud's writings made by his daughter Anna, the only one of his children to follow in his footsteps and also become a psychoanalyst

Two Short Accounts of Psychoanalysis, Penguin, A text based on the 1909 series of lectures given at Clark University in America and a 1926 text which makes clear the later revisions he made to his overall view of the mind and its workings, these are the most accessible of Freud's own writings to a general readership

The Complete Letters of Sigmund Freud to Wilhelm Fliess 1887 – 1904, Harvard UP, 1986, Only published in full in this edition, these letters between Freud and his closest intellectual confidant during the crucial years of the 1890s provide detailed insights into the early development of psychoanalysis

The Freud/Jung Letters, Princeton UP, 1974, The letters trace in fascinating detail the relationship between the two men from the promising beginning in 1906 to the embittered parting in 1913.

Biographies

Ernest Jones, *Sigmund Freud: Life and Work* (3 vols.), London, 1953-57. Jones' book has all the advantages and disadvantages of the best kind of 'official' biography of a great man. It was written by someone who had known Freud for more than thirty years and who had access to all the material that Freud's family wished to put at his disposal. It is exceptionally wide-ranging and packed with information. Yet, because of his closeness to Freud and the family, Jones is inclined to avoid criticism and, indeed, consciously omit material that might put his hero in a bad light. His book, however, remains essential reading for anyone with a serious interest in Freud.

Peter Gay, *Freud: A Life for Our Time*, London, 1988. Peter Gay is a very distinguished and erudite historian who has written a massive work on bourgeois culture in Europe during the nineteenth century. He is ideally placed both to position Freud's ideas historically and to draw out their continuing relevance decades after his death. His book is the most intellectually satisfying of modern biographies of Freud but assumes a certain prior knowledge of the subject.

Paul Ferris, *Dr. Freud: A Life*, Pimlico, 1998. The most lively modern biography for the non-specialist.

Studies

Anthony Storr, *Freud: A Very Short Introduction*, Oxford UP, 2001 (formerly one of the 'Past Masters' series) The best short introduction to Freud's work and its influence. Storr is a critical reader of Freud's writings and makes clear the lack of scientific backing for many of his ideas but, even at his most critical, he never loses sight of his subject's importance in the intellectual history of the last 100 years.

Richard Wollheim, *Freud*, (Modern Masters), Fontana, 1991. Another good short introduction to Freud's ideas.

David Stafford-Clark, *What Freud Really Said*, Penguin. Freud's ideas have been subject to much mangling and misinterpretation over the years. His own writings, of course, are the best place to go to encounter his thinking but these are, with some exceptions, quite daunting for a lay reader. Using generous quotations from the works, Stafford-Clark provides a readable introduction to what Freud really said.

Richard Appignanesi & Oscar Zarate, *Introducing Freud* (formerly called *Freud for Beginners*), Icon Books, 1999. One of an inventive collection of books which use a cartoon and comic-book style to introduce important thinkers and ideas. *Freud* was one of the first published in the series. Zarate's artwork and Appignanesi's text combine brilliantly and effectively to provide one of the most entertaining and clearly presented introductions to the subject.

Jerome Neu (ed), *The Cambridge Companion to Freud*, Cambridge UP, 1992. A collection of essays by academics in a number of fields who explore the continuing relevance of Freud's ideas in many disciplines.

Websites

http://freud.t0.or.at/freud/index-e.htm - The Website of the Sigmund Freud Museum in the house and consulting rooms at 19 Berggasse, Vienna where he lived for many years. The site is in English and includes a chronology of Freud's life, a virtual tour of the house and essays on psychoanalytic themes.

http://www.freud.org.uk - The Website of the Freud Museum in the house in Maresfield Gardens, Hampstead, London where Freud, having fled the Nazi regime in Austria, spent the last year of his life. Not very imaginatively presented but provides basic information about the house and Freud's time there.

http://www.freudpage.com/en-us/freud/index.html - Wide-ranging site which provides much information about Freud's life and work and about psychoanalysis in general. It also has a links page which leads through to many more Freud and psychoanalysis sites.

http://www.mii.kurume-u.ac.jp/~leuers/Freud.htm - Very extensive page of Freudian links.

http://nyfreudian.org/index.html - This is the official site of the New York Freudian Society and Psychoanalytic Training Institute and contains much material that is of relevance only to practising analysts but it also has abstracts of all Freud's major works on it.

The Essential Library: Currently Available

Film Directors:

Woody Allen (Revised) (£3.99)　　　Tim Burton (£3.99)
Jane Campion (£2.99)　　　John Carpenter (£3.99)
Jackie Chan (£2.99)　　　Joel & Ethan Coen (£3.99)
David Cronenberg (£3.99)　　　Terry Gilliam (£2.99)
Alfred Hitchcock (£3.99)　　　Krzysztof Kieslowski (£2.99)
Stanley Kubrick (£2.99)　　　Sergio Leone (£3.99)
David Lynch (£3.99)　　　Brian De Palma (£2.99)
Sam Peckinpah (£2.99)　　　Ridley Scott (£3.99)
Orson Welles (£2.99)　　　Billy Wilder (£3.99)
Steven Spielberg (£3.99)　　　Mike Hodges (£3.99)
Ang Lee (£3.99)

Film Genres:

Film Noir (£3.99)　　　Hong Kong's Heroic Bloodshed (£2.99)
Horror Films (£3.99)　　　Slasher Movies(£3.99)
Spaghetti Westerns (£3.99)　　　Vampire Films (£2.99)
Blaxploitation Films (£3.99)　　　Bollywood (£3.99)
French New Wave (£3.99)

Film Subjects:

Laurel & Hardy (£3.99)　　　Marx Brothers (£3.99)
Steve McQueen (£2.99)　　　Marilyn Monroe (£3.99)
The Oscars® (£3.99)　　　Filming On A Microbudget (£3.99)
Bruce Lee (£3.99)　　　Film Music (£3.99)

TV:

Doctor Who (£3.99)

Literature:

Cyberpunk (£3.99)　　　Philip K Dick (£3.99)
Agatha Christie (£3.99)　　　Noir Fiction (£2.99)
Terry Pratchett (£3.99)　　　Sherlock Holmes (£3.99)
Hitchhiker's Guide (Revised) (£3.99)

Ideas:

Conspiracy Theories (£3.99)　　　Nietzsche (£3.99)
Feminism (£3.99)

History:

Alchemy & Alchemists (£3.99)　　　The Crusades (£3.99)
American Civl War (£3.99)　　　American Indian Wars (£3.99)
The Black Death (£3.99)

Available at all good bookstores, or send a cheque to: **Pocket Essentials (Dept FP), 18 Coleswood Rd, Harpenden, Herts, AL5 1EQ, UK.** Please make cheques payable to 'Oldcastle Books.' Add 50p postage & packing for each book in the UK and £1 elsewhere.